BIBLE 300
Teacher's Guide

Author:
Alpha Omega Staff

Editor:
Alan Christopherson, M.S.

Alpha Omega
PUBLICATIONS

804 N. 2nd Ave. E.
Rock Rapids, IA 51246-1759

BIBLE 300

LIFEPAC® Overview

BIBLE SCOPE & SEQUENCE

	Grade 1	Grade 2	Grade 3
UNIT 1	GOD CREATED ALL THINGS • God created day and night • God created land and sea • God created plants and animals • God created people	WHO AM I? • God made us • God loves me • God helps me • God helped Daniel	LIVING FOR GOD • I love and obey God • I praise God • I worship God • I serve God
UNIT 2	GOD LOVES HIS CHILDREN • God cared for Shadrach, Meshach, and Abednego • God cared for Joash and Esther • God cares for His Children • God's children love Him	THE STORY OF MOSES • The early life of Moses • Life in Midian • Moses returns to Egypt • Life in the desert	THE LIFE OF JESUS CHRIST • Mary and Joseph • Jesus in the Temple • Jesus teaches and saves • Jesus dies and lives again
UNIT 3	WE CAN PRAY • We can ask and thank God • We can pray God's special prayer • God listens to us • We listen to God	GOD AND YOU • God is great • God keeps his promises • You should obey God • God rewards his people	GOD'S PLAN FOR JOSEPH • The dream of Joseph • Joseph and his brothers • Joseph in Egypt • God watched over Joseph
UNIT 4	GOD WANTS YOU TO BE GOOD • Jesus says love God • God says to love others • You show your love • God says to love yourself	HOW THE BIBLE CAME TO US • Moses and the Prophets • David and Solomon • The Apostles and Paul • Bible translators	YOU CAN USE THE BIBLE • The books of the Bible • How to read and study the Bible • How to find verses • How to memorize verses
UNIT 5	OLD TESTAMENT STORIES • Joseph, Elijah, Jonathan, and David • Miriam and Deborah • A rich woman and her son • Ishmael and Mephibosheth	DAVID'S SLING • David with the sheep • David and the prophet • David and Saul • David and the giant	GOD TAKES CARE OF HIS PEOPLE • God's love for people • God guides people • God protects people • God blesses people
UNIT 6	GOD'S PROMISE • God's Old Testament promises • God's promises kept • The birth of the Promised One • The life of the Promised One	GOD IS EVERYWHERE • Understanding the beginning • Understanding God • The creation • God's will	THE BIBLE IS GOD'S WORD • The writers of God's Word • God's Word is preserved • God's Word changes lives • Promises of God's Word
UNIT 7	JESUS, OUR SAVIOR • Jesus taught the people • Jesus healed the people • Jesus saves the people • Jesus will come again	THE STORY OF JOSEPH • Joseph as a boy at home • The worship of Joseph • Joseph in Egypt • Joseph and the famine	ARCHAEOLOGY AND THE BIBLE • The search for treasure • Clues from old stories • Explaining the puzzles • Joining the search
UNIT 8	GOD CALLS MISSIONARIES • The woman at the well • Stephen and Paul • Missionaries today • God calls missionaries	GOD AND THE FAMILY • The first family • Abraham's family • Happy families • God's promise to children	GOD GAVE US THE NEED FOR FRIENDS • We need love • We need friendship • God commands our love • Love for others
UNIT 9	NEW TESTAMENT STORIES • Lazarus, Thomas, Stephen • Mary, Anna, Lydia • Children in the New Testament • Jesus and the Children	GOD MADE THE NATIONS • The people of Babel • God's judgment at Babel • The new nation • Our big world	GOD'S PEOPLE HELP OTHERS • All people are created by God • God loves me • God's love to others • God is my Father
UNIT 10	GOD GAVE YOU MANY GIFTS • God created all things • God loves His children • God gave us His Word • God gave us His Son	GOD, HIS WORD, AND YOU • God as our Father • The Word of God • Life with God • Belonging to God	GOD'S WORD, JESUS, AND YOU • God speaks to Man • Writers of the Word • Jesus and the Word • God's family

BIBLE SCOPE & SEQUENCE

Grade 4	Grade 5	Grade 6	
HOW CAN I LIVE FOR GOD? • Peter found Jesus • Peter Fished for Men • To be born into God's family • To be fruitful through the Spirit	**HOW OTHERS LIVED FOR GOD** • Fellow-laborers with God • Abraham, a man of faith • Servants of God • Co-workers with God	**FROM CREATION TO MOSES** • Creation • The Flood • Abraham and his descendants • Moses and the Law	UNIT 1
GOD'S KNOWLEDGE • Knowledge to create • Learning God's knowledge • The benefits of God's knowledge • Using God's knowledge	**ANGELS** • Characteristics of Angels • Kinds of Angels • The ministry of Angels • Angels in the life of Jesus	**FROM JOSHUA TO SAMUEL** • Conquest and division of the land • The death of Joshua • The Judges of Israel • Ruth, Naomi, and Boaz	UNIT 2
SAUL BEGINS TO LIVE FOR GOD • Saul persecutes the Christians • God changes Saul • Saul preaches about Jesus • Paul belongs to Christ	**THE PRESENCE OF GOD** • Everywhere as God • Everywhere as a person • In the lives of people • In my life	**THE KINGDOM OF ISRAEL** • Samuel and Saul • The reign of David • The reign of Solomon • The books of poetry	UNIT 3
THE BIBLE AND ME • Reading and learning the Bible • Thinking about the Bible • Memorizing the Bible • Living the Bible way	**BIBLE METHODS AND STRUCTURE** • One book with many parts • Books of history • Books of poetry and prophecy • Books of the New Testament	**THE DIVIDED KINGDOM** • From Jeroboam to Captivity • Prophets of Judah and Israel • From Hezekiah to Captivity • Prophets of remaining kingdom	UNIT 4
GOD CARES FOR US • The Twenty-third Psalm • Jesus and the sheep • David as a shepherd • Daniel as a helper	**THE CHRISTIAN IN THE WORLD** • Instruction and correction • Learning correct behavior • Relationships at school • Relationships in the world	**CAPTIVITY AND RESTORATION** • The prophets of the captivity • The returns from exile • The prophets of the Restoration • Creation to Restoration	UNIT 5
HOW CAN I KNOW GOD EXISTS • God's plan for the Jews • A Jewish Savior • Man searches for God • Man needs God	**PROVING WHAT WE BELIEVE** • The Bible is God's Word • Evidence from the Bible • Evidence from history and science • Knowing that Christ arose	**THE LIFE OF JESUS** • Birth and background • The first years of ministry • The latter years of ministry • The death and Resurrection	UNIT 6
OLD TESTAMENT GEOGRAPHY • Bible Geography • Description of the Land • Abram's Nomadic Life • Abraham's Descendants	**MISSIONARY JOURNEYS OF PAUL** • Paul's background • Paul's missionary journeys • The Jerusalem Council • Paul's last years	**THE FOLLOWERS OF JESUS** • The disciples of Jesus • The friends of Jesus • Miracles of Jesus • The message of Jesus	UNIT 7
GOD-GIVEN WORTH • Who Am I? • God is my Creator • God is my Father • Knowing God's Love	**GOD CREATED MAN FOR ETERNITY** • Preparing for eternity • Christ is our Judge • The judgment of the Christian • The judgment of the unsaved	**THE APOSTLE PAUL** • Paul's background and conversion • Paul's missionary journeys • Paul's letters to churches • Paul's letters to people	UNIT 8
WITNESSING FOR JESUS • Loving God and Others • Following Jesus • Knowing who Jesus is • Following Paul's Example	**AUTHORITY AND LAW** • God is the source of law • The model of law • The authority of the family • Our authority of government	**HEBREWS AND GENERAL EPISTLES** • The book of Hebrews • James and 1st and 2nd Peter • The three Johns • The book of Jude	UNIT 9
GOD'S WAY IS PERFECT • Seeking Knowledge • Science & Geography • Living God's Way • Loving God's Way	**ANGELS, THE BIBLE, LIVING FOR GOD** • Presence of God and Angels • Understanding the Bible • Areas of service • The order of authority	**REVELATION AND REVIEW** • The Lord Jesus in Revelation • End-time events • Old Testament review • New Testament review	UNIT 10

BIBLE SCOPE & SEQUENCE

	Grade 7	Grade 8	Grade 9
UNIT 1	**WORSHIP** • The nature of worship • Old Testament worship • New Testament worship • True worship	**PRAYER** • Organization of the Lord's Prayer • Purpose of the Lord's Prayer • History of prayer • Practical use of prayer	**THE NEW TESTAMENT** • Inter-Testamental period • Pharisees and Sadducees • New Testament themes • New Testament events
UNIT 2	**MANKIND** • The origin of man • The fall of man • The re-creation of man • The mission of man	**SIN AND SALVATION** • The nature of sin • The need for salvation • How to receive salvation • The results of salvation	**THE GOSPELS** • Matthew • Mark • Luke • John
UNIT 3	**THE ATTRIBUTES OF GOD** • God's nature of love • God's expression of love • The mercy of God • The grace of God	**ATTRIBUTES OF GOD** • God's justice • God's immutability • God's eternal nature • God's love	**THE ACTS OF THE APOSTLES** • The writer • The purpose • Pentecost • Missions
UNIT 4	**FULFILLED PROPHECIES OF CHRIST** • Method of the First Advent • Purpose of the First Advent • The Messiah foretold • Fulfillment of the Messiah	**EARLY CHURCH LEADERS** • The early church • The church of the Middle Ages • The Renaissance • The Reformation	**THE PAULINE EPISTLES** • Paul as a person • The early epistles • Prison epistles • The later epistles
UNIT 5	**LIVING THE BALANCED LIFE** • The Father's gift of life • Man's deception • Fellowship with the Savior • The life of the Spirit	**EARLY CHURCH HISTORY** • The Roman Empire • The background of the Jews • The ministry of Jesus • The Jerusalem church	**GENERAL EPISTLES** • James • First and Second Peter • First, Second, and Third John • Hebrews and Jude
UNIT 6	**THE PSALMS** • The history of the Psalms • Types of Psalms • Hebrew poetry • Psalm 100	**THE EARLY CHURCHES** • The church at Antioch • The missionary journeys • The Jerusalem Conference • New Testament churches	**THE REVELATION OF JESUS CHRIST** • The seven churches • The seven seals and trumpets • The seven signs and plagues • The seven judgments and wonders
UNIT 7	**THE LIFE OF CHRIST: PART ONE** • Early life of Christ • Christ's ministry begins • The early Judean ministry • The early Galilean ministry	**THE BOOK OF PROVERBS** • Literary forms and outline • Objectives and purposes • Influence on the New Testament • Key themes	**JOB AND SUFFERING** • The scenes of Job • Attitudes toward suffering • Christ's suffering on Earth • The victory of Christ's suffering
UNIT 8	**THE LIFE OF CHRIST: PART TWO** • The public ministry in Galilee • The private ministry in Galilee • The Judean ministry • The Perean ministry	**TODAY'S PROBLEMS** • Guidance for behavior • Characteristics of friendship • Studying effectively • Finding God's will	**HOW TO SHARE CHRIST** • Personal evangelism • Outreach to others • Personal and family missions • Assisting a missionary
UNIT 9	**THE LIFE OF CHRIST: PART THREE** • Jesus' final ministry • Jesus' suffering and crucifixion • Jesus' resurrection and ascension	**UNDERSTANDING PARENTS** • Human parents • Biblical parents • Children's responsibility • Parents and children as a team	**GOD'S WILL FOR MY LIFE** • The desire of the heart • The Word and work of God • Importance of goals • The use of talents
UNIT 10	**IN SUMMARY** • The plan of God • Man's history • The Savior's solution • Worship of Christ	**WALKING WITH GOD** • Prayer and salvation • The attributes of God • The early church leaders • Christian living	**THE WALK WITH CHRIST** • Background of the New Testament • The Epistles and Revelation • The importance of suffering • God's will for my life

BIBLE SCOPE & SEQUENCE

Grade 10	Grade 11	Grade 12	
CREATION TO ABRAHAM • The six days of creation • The fall of man • Noah and his descendants • Nations of the earth	**THE FAITHFULNESS OF GOD** • Affirmation of God's faithfulness • Nature of God's faithfulness • Manifestations of God's faithfulness • Implications of God's faithfulness	**KNOWING YOURSELF** • Your creation by God • Interacting with others • A child and servant of God • Your personal skills	UNIT 1
ABRAHAM TO MOSES • Abraham's call and promise • The covenant with Isaac • The life of Jacob • Joseph and his family	**ROMANS: PART ONE** • The Roman Empire and Church • The book of Romans • Paul's message to the Romans • Sin and salvation in Romans	**CHRISTIAN MINISTRIES** • Christian ministry defined • Church related ministries • Other ministries • A ministry as a career	UNIT 2
EXODUS AND WANDERINGS • The journey to Sinai • The giving of the Law • Numbering the people • The book of Deuteronomy	**ROMANS: PART TWO** • The chosen of God • Service and submission • From sin to salvation • The victory of salvation	**CHOOSING A CHRISTIAN MINISTRY** • Where to look for a ministry • What to look for in a ministry • How to look for a ministry • Choosing a ministry for a career	UNIT 3
ISRAEL IN CANAAN • Preparing for battle • The fight for the land • Dividing the land • The death of Joshua	**THE DOCTRINE OF JESUS CHRIST** • Identity and incarnation of Christ • The individuality of Christ • Christ's work on the Cross • Christ's work after the Cross	**GODHEAD** • Old Testament view • New Testament view • Historical Perspectives • Faith and man's relationship	UNIT 4
THE JUDGES AND SPIRITUAL DECLINE • Background of Judges • History of the Judges • Examples of spiritual decay • Ruth and redemption	**THE NATION OF ISRAEL** • The covenant with Abraham • Israel as a nation • Old Testament archaeology • New Testament archaeology	**ATTRIBUTES OF GOD** • The Holiness of God • The Goodness of God • Holiness and the believer • Goodness and the Creation	UNIT 5
THE KINGDOM • Samuel and Saul • David • Solomon • Hebrew poetry	**HISTORY OF THE CANON** • Revelation and inspiration • Illumination and interpretation • Authority of the Bible • Formation of the Bible	**THE EPISTLES OF JAMES AND JOHN** • James, the man • The message of James • John, the man • The message of John's epistles	UNIT 6
THE DIVIDED KINGDOM • Jeroboam to Ahab • Ahab to Jehu • Jehu to Assyrian captivity • Prophets of the period	**FRIENDSHIP, DATING, AND MARRIAGE** • Meaning and role of friendship • Perspectives of dating • Principles of relationships • The structure of marriage	**DANIEL** • A man of conviction • An interpreter of dreams • A watchman in prayer • A man of visions	UNIT 7
THE REMAINING KINGDOM • The time of Hezekiah • Manasseh to Josiah • Jehoahaz to the exile • Prophets of the period	**THE PURSUIT OF HAPPINESS** • Solomon's succession • Solomon's prosperity • Solomon's fall • Solomon's reflection	**COMPARATIVE RELIGIONS** • Elements of Christianity • The validity of Christian faith • World religions • The occult	UNIT 8
THE CAPTIVITY • Prophets of the period • Jeremiah • Ezekiel • Daniel	**ANSWERS FOR AGNOSTICS** • Integrity of the Bible • Doctrines of the Bible • Interpretation of the Bible • Application of the Bible	**WISDOM FOR TODAY'S YOUTH** • Life and character of David • Life and riches of Solomon • Psalms and Proverbs • The Bible and literature	LIFEPAC 9
THE RESTORATION • First return from exile • The Jews preserved • Second return from exile • Haggai, Zechariah, and Malachi	**GOD, HIS WORD, AND THE CHRISTIAN** • The uniqueness of the Bible • History of Israel • God revealed in the Bible • Principles for living	**PRACTICAL CHRISTIAN LIVING** • Christian fundamentals • Growing in Christian maturity • A ministry for Christ • A testimony for Christ	UNIT 10

STRUCTURE OF THE LIFEPAC CURRICULUM

The LIFEPAC curriculum is conveniently structured to provide one teacher's guide containing teacher support material with answer keys and ten student worktexts for each subject at grade levels two through twelve. The worktext format of the LIFEPACs allows the student to read the textual information and complete workbook activities all in the same booklet. The easy-to-follow LIFEPAC numbering system lists the grade as the first number(s) and the last two digits as the number of the series. For example, the Language Arts LIFEPAC at the 6th grade level, 5th book in the series would be LAN0605.

Each LIFEPAC is divided into 3 to 5 sections and begins with an introduction or overview of the booklet as well as a series of specific learning objectives to give a purpose to the study of the LIFEPAC. The introduction and objectives are followed by a vocabulary section which may be found at the beginning of each section at the lower levels or in the glossary at the high school level. Vocabulary words are used to develop word recognition and should not be confused with the spelling words introduced later in the LIFEPAC. The student should learn all vocabulary words before working the LIFEPAC sections to improve comprehension, retention, and reading skills.

Each activity or written assignment in grades 2 through 12 has a number for easy identification, such as 1.1. The first number corresponds to the LIFEPAC section and the number to the right of the decimal is the number of the activity.

Teacher checkpoints, which are essential to maintain quality learning, are found at various locations throughout the LIFEPAC. The teacher should check 1) neatness of work and penmanship, 2) quality of understanding (tested with a short oral quiz), 3) thoroughness of answers (complete sentences and paragraphs, correct spelling, etc.), 4) completion of activities (no blank spaces), and 5) accuracy of answers as compared to the answer key (all answers correct).

The self test questions in grades 2 through 12 are also number coded for easy reference. For example, 2.015 means that this is the 15th question in the self test of Section 2. The first number corresponds to the LIFEPAC section, the zero indicates that it is a self test question, and the number to the right of the zero the question number.

The LIFEPAC test is packaged at the center of each LIFEPAC. It should be removed and put aside before giving the booklet to the student for study.

Answer and test keys in grades 2 through 12 have the same numbering system as the LIFEPACs. The student may be given access to the answer keys (not the test keys) under teacher supervision so that he can score his own work.

A thorough study of the Scope & Sequence by the teacher before instruction begins is essential to the success of the student. The teacher should become familiar with expected skill mastery and understand how these grade-level skills fit into the overall skill development of the curriculum. The teacher should also preview the objectives that appear at the beginning of each LIFEPAC for additional preparation and planning.

TEST SCORING AND GRADING

Answer keys and test keys give examples of correct answers. They convey the idea, but the student may use many ways to express a correct answer. The teacher should check for the essence of the answer, not for the exact wording. Many questions are high level and require thinking and creativity on the part of the student. Each answer should be scored based on whether or not the main idea written by the student matches the model example. "Any Order" or "Either Order" in a key indicates that no particular order is necessary to be correct.

Most self tests and LIFEPAC tests at the lower elementary levels are scored at 1 point per answer; however, the upper levels may have a point system awarding 2 to 5 points for various answers or questions. Further, the total test points will vary; they may not always equal 100 points. They may be 78, 85, 100, 105, etc.

Example 1

Example 2

A score box similar to ex. 1 above is located at the end of each self test and on the front of the LIFEPAC test. The bottom score, 72, represents the total number of points possible on the test. The upper score, 58, represents the number of points your student will need to receive an 80% or passing grade. If you wish to establish the exact percentage that your student has achieved, find the total points of his correct answers and divide it by the bottom number (in this case, 72). For example, if your student has a point total of 65, divide 65 by 72 for a grade of 90%. Referring to ex. 2, on a test with a total of 105 possible points, the student would have to receive a minimum of 84 correct points for an 80% or passing grade. If your student has received 93 points, simply divide the 93 by 105 for a percentage grade of 89%. Students who receive a score below 80% should review the LIFEPAC and retest using the appropriate Alternate Test found in the Teacher's Guide.

The following is a guideline to assign letter grades for completed LIFEPACs based on a maximum total score of 100 points.

Example:

LIFEPAC Test	=	60% of the Total Score (or percent grade)
Self Test	=	25% of the Total Score (average percent of self tests)
Reports	=	10% or 10* points per LIFEPAC
Oral Work	=	5% or 5* points per LIFEPAC

*Determined by the teacher's subjective evaluation of the student's daily work.

Example:

LIFEPAC Test Score	=	92%	$92 \times .60$ =	55 points
Self Test Average	=	90%	$90 \times .25$ =	23 points
Reports			=	8 points
Oral Work			=	4 points

TOTAL POINTS	=	90 points

Grade Scale based on point system:

100 – 94	=	A
93 – 86	=	B
85 – 77	=	C
76 – 70	=	D
Below 70	=	F

TEACHER HINTS AND STUDYING TECHNIQUES

LIFEPAC activities are written to check the level of understanding of the preceding text. The student may look back to the text as necessary to complete these activities; however, a student should never attempt to do the activities without reading (studying) the text first. Self tests and LIFEPAC tests are never open book tests.

Language arts activities (skill integration) often appear within other subject curriculum. The purpose is to give the student an opportunity to test his skill mastery outside of the context in which it was presented. Writing complete answers (paragraphs) to some questions is an integral part of the LIFEPAC curriculum in all subjects. This builds communication and organization skills, increases understanding and retention of ideas, and helps enforce good penmanship. Complete sentences should be encouraged for this type of activity. Obviously, single words or phrases do not meet the intent of the activity, since multiple lines are given for the response.

Review is essential to student success. Time invested in review where review is suggested will be time saved in correcting errors later. Self tests, unlike the section activities, are closed book. This procedure helps to identify weaknesses before they become too great to overcome. Certain objectives from self tests are cumulative and test previous sections; therefore, good preparation for a self test must include all material studied up to that testing point.

The following procedure checklist has been found to be successful in developing good study habits in the LIFEPAC curriculum.

1. Read the introduction and Table of Contents.
2. Read the objectives.
3. Recite and study the entire vocabulary (glossary) list.
4. Study each section as follows:
   a. Read the introduction and study the section objectives.
   b. Read all the text for the entire section, but answer none of the activities.
   c. Return to the beginning of the section and memorize each vocabulary word and definition.
   d. Reread the section, complete the activities, check the answers with the answer key, correct all errors, and have the teacher check.
   e. Read the self test but do not answer the questions.
   f. Go to the beginning of the first section and reread the text and answers to the activities up to the self test you have not yet done.
   g. Answer the questions to the self test without looking back.
   h. Have the self test checked by the teacher.
   i. Correct the self test and have the teacher check the corrections.
   j. Repeat steps a–i for each section.
5. Use the SQ3R method to prepare for the LIFEPAC test.

   Scan the whole LIFEPAC.
   Question yourself on the objectives.
   Read the whole LIFEPAC again.
   Recite through an oral examination.
   Review weak areas.

6. Take the LIFEPAC test as a closed book test.
7. LIFEPAC tests are administered and scored under direct teacher supervision. Students who receive scores below 80% should review the LIFEPAC using the SQ3R study method and take the Alternate Test located in the Teacher's Guide. The final test grade may be the grade on the Alternate Test or an average of the grades from the original LIFEPAC test and the Alternate Test

GOAL SETTING AND SCHEDULES

Each school must develop its own schedule, because no single set of procedures will fit every situation. The following is an example of a daily schedule that includes the five LIFEPAC subjects as well as time slotted for special activities.

Possible Daily Schedule

8:15	–	8:25	Pledges, prayer, songs, devotions, etc.
8:25	–	9:10	Bible
9:10	–	9:55	Language Arts
9:55	–	10:15	Recess (juice break)
10:15	–	11:00	Math
11:00	–	11:45	History & Geography
11:45	–	12:30	Lunch, recess, quiet time
12:30	–	1:15	Science
1:15	–		Drill, remedial work, enrichment*

*__Enrichment:__ *Computer time, physical education, field trips, fun reading, games and puzzles, family business, hobbies, resource persons, guests, crafts, creative work, electives, music appreciation, projects.*

Basically, two factors need to be considered when assigning work to a student in the LIFEPAC curriculum.

The first is time. An average of 45 minutes should be devoted to each subject, each day. Remember, this is only an average. Because of extenuating circumstances a student may spend only 15 minutes on a subject one day and the next day spend 90 minutes on the same subject.

The second factor is the number of pages to be worked in each subject. A single LIFEPAC is designed to take three to four weeks to complete. Allowing about three to four days for LIFEPAC introduction, review, and tests, the student has approximately 15 days to complete the LIFEPAC pages. Simply take the number of pages in the LIFEPAC, divide it by 15 and you will have the number of pages that must be completed on a daily basis to keep the student on schedule. For example, a LIFEPAC containing 45 pages will require three completed pages per day. Again, this is only an average. While working a 45-page LIFEPAC, the student may complete only one page the first day if the text has a lot of activities or reports, but go on to complete five pages the next day.

Long range planning requires some organization. Because the traditional school year originates in the early fall of one year and continues to late spring of the following year, a calendar should be devised that covers this period of time. Approximate beginning and completion dates can be noted on the calendar as well as special occasions such as holidays, vacations and birthdays. Since each LIFEPAC takes three to four weeks or 18 days to complete, it should take about 180 school days to finish a set of ten LIFEPACs. Starting at the beginning school date, mark off 18 school days on the calendar and that will become the targeted completion date for the first LIFEPAC. Continue marking the calendar until you have established dates for the remaining nine LIFEPACs making adjustments for previously noted holidays and vacations. If all five subjects are being used, the ten established target dates should be the same for the LIFEPACs in each subject.

TEACHING SUPPLEMENTS

The sample weekly lesson plan and student grading sheet forms are included in this section as teacher support materials and may be duplicated at the convenience of the teacher.

The student grading sheet is provided for those who desire to follow the suggested guidelines for assignment of letter grades as previously discussed. The student's self test scores should be posted as percentage grades. When the LIFEPAC is completed the teacher should average the self test grades, multiply the average by .25 and post the points in the box marked self test points. The LIFEPAC percentage grade should be multiplied by .60 and posted. Next, the teacher should award and post points for written reports and oral work. A report may be any type of written work assigned to the student whether it is a LIFEPAC or additional learning activity. Oral work includes the student's ability to respond orally to questions which may or may not be related to LIFEPAC activities or any type of oral report assigned by the teacher. The points may then be totaled and a final grade entered along with the date that the LIFEPAC was completed.

The Student Record Book, which was specifically designed for use with the Alpha Omega curriculum, provides space to record weekly progress for one student over a nine-week period as well as a place to post self test and LIFEPAC scores. The Student Record Books are available through the current Alpha Omega catalog; however, unlike the enclosed forms these books are not for duplication and should be purchased in sets of four to cover a full academic year.

WEEKLY LESSON PLANNER

Week of:

	Subject	Subject	Subject	Subject
Monday				
Tuesday	Subject	Subject	Subject	Subject
Wednesday	Subject	Subject	Subject	Subject
Thursday	Subject	Subject	Subject	Subject
Friday	Subject	Subject	Subject	Subject

WEEKLY LESSON PLANNER

Week of:

	Subject	Subject	Subject	Subject
Monday				
Tuesday	Subject	Subject	Subject	Subject
Wednesday	Subject	Subject	Subject	Subject
Thursday	Subject	Subject	Subject	Subject
Friday	Subject	Subject	Subject	Subject

Student Name _____   Year _____

Bible

LP	Self Test Scores by Sections					Self Test Points	LIFEPAC Test	Oral Points	Report Points	Final Grade	Date
	1	2	3	4	5						
01											
02											
03											
04											
05											
06											
07											
08											
09											
10											

History & Geography

LP	Self Test Scores by Sections					Self Test Points	LIFEPAC Test	Oral Points	Report Points	Final Grade	Date
	1	2	3	4	5						
01											
02											
03											
04											
05											
06											
07											
08											
09											
10											

Language Arts

LP	Self Test Scores by Sections					Self Test Points	LIFEPAC Test	Oral Points	Report Points	Final Grade	Date
	1	2	3	4	5						
01											
02											
03											
04											
05											
06											
07											
08											
09											
10											

Student Name _____   Year _____

Math

LP	Self Test Scores by Sections					Self Test Points	LIFEPAC Test	Oral Points	Report Points	Final Grade	Date
	1	2	3	4	5						
01											
02											
03											
04											
05											
06											
07											
08											
09											
10											

Science

LP	Self Test Scores by Sections					Self Test Points	LIFEPAC Test	Oral Points	Report Points	Final Grade	Date
	1	2	3	4	5						
01											
02											
03											
04											
05											
06											
07											
08											
09											
10											

Spelling/Electives

LP	Self Test Scores by Sections					Self Test Points	LIFEPAC Test	Oral Points	Report Points	Final Grade	Date
	1	2	3	4	5						
01											
02											
03											
04											
05											
06											
07											
08											
09											
10											

INSTRUCTIONS FOR BIBLE

The LIFEPAC curriculum from grades 2 through 12 is structured so that the daily instructional material is written directly into the LIFEPACs. The student is encouraged to read and follow this instructional material in order to develop independent study habits. The teacher should introduce the LIFEPAC to the student, set a required completion schedule, complete teacher checks, be available for questions regarding both content and procedures, administer and grade tests, and develop additional learning activities as desired. Teachers working with several students may schedule their time so that students are assigned to a quiet work activity when it is necessary to spend instructional time with one particular student.

The Teacher Notes section of the guide lists the required or suggested materials for the LIFEPACs and provides additional learning activities for the students. The materials section refers only to LIFEPAC materials and does not include materials which may be needed for the additional activities. Additional learning activities provide a change from the daily school routine, encourage the student's interest in learning and may be used as a reward for good study habits.

BIBLE 301

Unit 1: Living for God

TEACHER NOTES

MATERIALS NEEDED FOR LIFEPAC	
Required	Suggested
(None)	• Bible • crayons • water colors • scissors • Biblical pictures • drawing paper • newsprint • paste • light cardboard

ADDITIONAL LEARNING ACTIVITIES

Section 1: Loving and Obeying God

1. Discuss these questions with your class.

   a. Do you know anyone without children?

   b. What was the land like where Abraham lived?

   c. Who will be your descendants?

   d. Do you think God tests people today?

   e. What rules do you obey?

   f. Who do you not obey?

   g. How do you show love?

2. Have a rabbi speak to the class about Abraham.

3. Make a list of the rules that students feel are to be obeyed at school.

4. Show a film on the life of Abraham.

5. Read more stories about Abraham.

6. Read about Bible times in other books.

7. Write a story about obeying.

8. Make a class presentation of the Abraham story.

Section 2: Loving and Praising God

1. Discuss these questions.

   a. What missionaries do you know?

   b. Are missionaries ever put in jail?

   c. Have you ever been in an earthquake?

2. Enact the story of the girl with Paul and Silas.

3. Draw pictures of the story to be put up in the room.

4. Write more songs of praise.

5. Use hymnals to make a list of hymns praising God.

6. Read more about things that happened to Paul.

7. Make a map of Paul's trips.

8. Find out more about the customs of the people where Paul went.
   Write the facts in an interesting report to be read in class.

Section 3: Loving and Worshiping God

1. Discuss these questions.

   a. Why would anyone worship a statue?

   b. How did the people live who were with Moses?

   c. Can you find the location of Mount Sinai on the map?

   d. What do you think it would be like to talk to God as Moses did on the mountain?

2. Study and learn the Ten Commandments.

3. Draw a big map of the trip in the wilderness.

4. Talk about transportation in those days.

5. Discuss the conveniences of today.

6. Discuss being patient and impatient.

7. Write stories about worship of something other than the true God.

8. Read accounts of other religions.

Section 4: Loving and Serving God

1. Discuss these questions with your class.

   a. How would you feel if you had to pray to a person?

   b. Is it sometimes easy or hard to do what God wants?

   c. Do you often have to make decisions about whether to follow God's rules?

   d. Even if no one else knows, should you follow God's rules?

2. Discuss decisions that everyone has to make about serving God.

3. Write a class story together about serving God.

4. Play questions and answers like a spelling bee about facts from the LIFEPAC.

5. Help students to write and produce a play about a young person who has to make
   a decision about obeying God.

6. Develop a program with an announcer telling the public about Daniel and the commotion
   that occurred. Present the program to the class with some of the members enacting the
   sequence.

Administer the LIFEPAC Test.

ANSWER KEYS

SECTION 1

1.1	miracle
1.2	Isaac
1.3	Sarah
1.4	loved
1.5	descendants
1.6	loved Him
1.7	a sacrifice
1.8	a gift for God
1.9	love for God
1.10	son
1.11	lamb or calf
1.12	the lamb
1.13	God
1.14	angel of the Lord
1.15	a ram
1.16	happy face
	happy face
	sad face
	sad face
	happy face
1.17	(afraid,) (fearful) (sad,) (surprised)
1.18	to test his love
1.19	dis re re dis
	in un in un
1.20	1. sacrifice
	2. Abraham
	3. altar
	4. obeyed
	5. Isaac
	6. test
	7. lamb
1.21	love, obey
1.22	love, obey
1.23	love, obey
1.24	love, obey

SELF TEST 1

1.01	a. (Isaac)
1.02	c. (lamb)
1.03	c. (God)
1.04	b. (obeying God)
1.05	c. (test)
1.06	no
1.07	yes
1.08	yes
1.09	no
1.010	no
1.011	became the real sacrifice
1.012	provided a ram for the sacrifice
1.013	asked where the lamb was
1.014	obeyed God
1.015	stopped Abraham from killing his son

SECTION 2

2.1	b.	put them in stocks.
2.2	c.	beaten.
2.3	d.	praising God.
2.4	c.	at all times.
2.5	d.	had everything under control.

2.6   2

        4

        5

        3

        1

        6

2.7   "What must I do to be saved?"

2.8   "I command thee in the name of Jesus to come out of her."

2.9   "These men are bringing trouble to our city."

2.10 "These men are servants of the most high God."

2.11 disobey—to not do as told

       unkind—not nice

       inside—being within

       uncover—find

       unselfish—giving, caring for others

2.12 I will bless the Lord at all times: His praise shall continually be in my mouth.

2.13 answers will vary

SELF TEST 2

2.01	Isaac
2.02	jailer
2.03	girl
2.04	Abraham
2.05	Silas
2.06	miracle
2.07	obeyed
2.08	praise
2.09	praised
2.010	sacrifice
2.011	miracle
2.012	praised
2.013	love
2.014	bless, Lord, all times, praise, in, mouth

SECTION 3

3.1   1. Wicked
        2. One
        3. Right
        4. Sang
        5. Home
        6. Impatient
        7. People
        8. Golden calf
        9. Obey
        10. Days

3.2   God

3.3   hear

3.4   see

3.5   worshiping

3.6   yes

3.7   yes

3.8   no

3.9   no

3.10 yes

3.11

spring	spray
spread	spread
spray	spruce
sprout	spring
spruce	sprout

3.12

string	strong
stray	stream
stream	stripe
stripe	string
strong	stray

3.13 baseball

SELF TEST 3

3.01 praising, obeying, worshiping

3.02 praising

3.03 obeying

3.04 worshiping

3.05 Moses

3.06 Abraham

3.07 Paul

3.08 Moses

3.09 Abraham

3.010 We spent part of a night praising God in jail.

3.011 I called two men "servants of God."

3.012 I was made by Aaron.

3.013 We worshiped the golden calf instead of the true God.

3.014 My praises to God are now in a book of the Bible.

3.015 The jailer learned this after an earthquake.

3.016 We are Abraham's descendants.

3.017 This happened to three thousand Israelite men because they didn't worship God.

3.018 Abraham chose to do this because he loved God.

3.019 Moses talked to God for forty days.

SECTION 4

4.1 Israelite
4.2 honest
4.3 Babylon
4.4 Israel
4.5 serving
4.6 ruler
4.7 jealous
4.8 wrong
4.9 king
4.10 liked
4.11 yes
4.12 no
4.13 no
4.14 yes
4.15 yes
4.16 the king
4.17 the king
4.18 Daniel
4.19 wicked man
4.20 the king
4.21 answers will vary
4.22 wild
4.23 child
4.24 mild
4.25 mind
4.26 find
4.27 blind
4.28 grind
4.29 kind
4.30 love
4.31 serve
4.32 love, serve

SELF TEST 4

4.01 Abraham
4.02 Paul and Silas
4.03 Daniel
4.04 the golden calf
4.05 an Israelite
4.06 Babylon
4.07 were jealous of Daniel
4.08 the wicked men
4.09 worshiping a golden calf
4.010 Abraham and Sarah
4.011 Paul and Silas
4.012 The wicked men
4.013 The girl
4.014 Paul
4.015 jealous
4.016 angry
4.017 happy
4.018 an earthquake
4.019 a ram
4.020 Abraham
4.021 5, 3, 1, 4, 2

LIFEPAC TEST

1. Example: they loved God and knew He would take care of them
2. he loved Him
3. God, the king
4. the golden calf
5. Isaac
6. Moses
7. Daniel
8. Examples: Isaac's birth, earthquake, healing servant girl, Daniel saved from lion's den
9. Lord
10. praise

11. – 14. Any order:

11. obey
12. praise
13. worship
14. serve
15. "I was promised to my father and mother by God."
16. "Paul and I sang praises to God in prison."
17. "The Lord saved me from the lions' mouths."
18. "I loved Daniel and didn't want to see him die."
19. "My friends and I were killed by lions."
20. "God gave me power to cast out a bad spirit."
21. "I obeyed God and was willing to sacrifice my only son."
22. "I was healed of a bad spirit."
23. "I talked with God on the mountain."
24. "I wrote many praises to God, and they are now called psalms."
25. Son
26. God
27. David
28. praise
29. Moses
30. Worshiping the golden calf
31. The Israelites
32. worship a golden calf

ALTERNATE LIFEPAC TEST

1. Psalms
2. Moses
3. the true God
4. miracle
5. love
6. impatient
7. disobey Him
8. an Israelite
9. Lord
10. Isaac, or his son
11. praise
12. God
13. God
14. loved
15. a golden calf
16. praise
17. mountain
18. lions
19. obey God
20. praise God
21. worship God
22. serve God
23. Aaron—made a golden calf
24. Moses—talked to God on the mountain
25. David—wrote praises to God in psalms
26. Abraham—was willing to sacrifice his son
27. Paul—healed a girl in the name of Jesus
28. jailer—heard about Jesus from Paul and Silas
29. the king—didn't want to see Daniel killed
30. Daniel—was saved from lions by God
31. Silas—sang praises to God in prison with Paul
32. Isaac—promised by God to his father and mother

BIBLE 301

ALTERNATE LIFEPAC TEST

NAME _____

DATE _____

SCORE _____

26

32

Each answer = 1 point

Circle the correct words.

1. David wrote praises to God in the Bible Book of _____ .
    a. Matthew
    b. Psalms
    c. Genesis

2. The leader of the Israelites was _____ .
    a. Abraham
    b. David
    c. Moses

3. Daniel worshiped _____ .
    a. the true God
    b. a golden calf
    c. an idol

4. Isaac's birth was a _____ .
    a. sacrifice
    b. miracle
    c. psalm

5. When you obey God, you are showing your _____ .
    a. miracle
    b. life
    c. love

6. If you are not willing to wait you are _____ .
    a. impossible
    b. impatient
    c. inactive

7. One way *not* to show love to God is to _____ .
    a. disobey Him
    b. praise Him
    c. serve Him

8. Daniel was _____ .
    a. Abraham's son
    b. the king's son
    c. an Israelite

Write the missing words in the blanks.

9. "I will bless the _____ at all times."

10. Because he wanted to obey God, Abraham was willing to sacrifice _____ .

11. The word *magnify* means to _____ .

12. When Paul and Silas were in jail, they praised _____ .

13. Daniel chose to pray to _____ .

14. Abraham obeyed God because he _____ God.

15. When Moses was on the mountain, the Israelites worshiped _____ .

16. "His _____ shall continually be in my mouth."

17. Sinai was a _____ .

18. Daniel was thrown into a den of _____ .

Write the four ways you have learned to show your love to God.

19. _____
_____

20. _____
_____

21. _____
_____

22. _____
_____

Draw a line to match the person with what he did.

23. Aaron ●
24. Moses ●
25. David ●
26. Abraham ●
27. Paul ●
28. jailer ●
29. the king ●
30. Daniel ●
31. Silas ●
32. Isaac ●

a. was saved from lions by God
b. was willing to sacrifice his son
c. promised by God to his father and mother
d. heard about Jesus from Paul and Silas
e. healed a girl in the name of Jesus
f. sang praises to God in prison with Paul
g. wrote praises to God in psalms
h. talked to God on the mountain
i. didn't want to see Daniel killed
j. made a golden calf

BIBLE 302

Unit 2: The Life of Jesus Christ

TEACHER NOTES

MATERIALS NEEDED FOR LIFEPAC	
Required	Suggested
(None)	• Bible • crayons • water colors • scissors • Biblical pictures • drawing paper • newsprint • paste • light cardboard • cardboard box • dowels (2) • banner paper • paste • digital recording device

ADDITIONAL LEARNING ACTIVITIES

Section 1: Jesus Is Born

1. Discuss these questions with your class.

    a. What do you think Gabriel looked like?

    b. Can you find Nazareth on a map?

    c. Who was the important relative of Mary and Joseph?

    d. Can you see the Holy Spirit?

    e. Where is Bethlehem?

    f. How would the shepherds feel when they saw an angel?

    g. Why do people pay taxes?

2. Invite a speaker to tell the class about his trip to the Holy Land.

3. Enact the trip from Nazareth to Bethlehem.

4. Write about a boy who lived in Bethlehem when the many people came to be taxed.

5. Read other books about these happenings.

6. Write a play about one of these happenings.

7. Write a story using the Vocabulary.

Section 2: Jesus Is a Boy

1. Discuss these questions with your class.

   a. How far is it from Nazareth to Jerusalem?

   b. Why did the family go to Jerusalem each year?

   c. How would you feel if someone were lost in your family?

   d. What do you think Jesus discussed in the temple?

   e. Where was the temple?

   f. Is the temple there today?

2. Show films of the Holy Land.

3. Make a moving-pictures drawing account of the temple story using a big box, rolls of paper for the pictures, and dowels for winding the paper. Cut a hole in the box for viewing the pictures as they pass by when the dowels are turned.

4. Make a relief map of the Holy Land with salt dough.

5. Write a song telling about Jesus in the temple.

6. Write a modern-day story of Jesus in the temple.

Section 3: Jesus Is a Man

1. Discuss these questions.

   a. Where did Jesus heal the sick people?

   b. Would you have gone to see Him?

   c. Where is the Jordan River?

   d. Why did Jesus choose the disciples?

   e. How do you find out about Jesus today?

2. Have a doctor speak to the class about unexplained healings that he believes God alone cured.

3. Make a class mural showing crowds watching Jesus heal someone.

4. Discuss other Bible stories about the ministry of Jesus that are not included in this LIFEPAC.

5. Make a recording of the dialogue in one of the stories in this part of the life of Jesus.

6. Play the recording for the class and have the class illustrate the recording with hand paintings. The students who need independent activities could edit and show the final product.

Section 4: Jesus Is the Son of God

1. Discuss these questions with your class.

    a. Why was Jesus in Jerusalem?

    b. What event did the Passover honor?

    c. Who wanted Jesus killed?

    d. Why was he thought to be an enemy of the Jewish leaders?

    e. What did the women think they would find at the tomb?

    f. What was different about the death of Jesus?

    g. What promise did He give His disciples?

2. Attend a Jewish service.

3. Have a rabbi speak to the class about the Passover.

4. Plan a sunrise service if possible to demonstrate what the daytime was like when the women went to the tomb.

5. Interview ministers about the importance of the empty tomb.

6. Write a story of a child who lived in Nazareth and played with Jesus.

Administer the LIFEPAC Test.

The test is to be administered in one session. Give no help except with directions.
Evaluate the tests and review areas where the students have done poorly.
Review the pages and activities that stress the concepts tested.
If necessary, administer the Alternate LIFEPAC Test.

ANSWER KEYS

SECTION 1

1.1	God
1.2	Savior
1.3	virgin
1.4	Savior
1.5	Joseph
1.6	engaged
1.7	b. Gabriel
1.8	d. Mary
1.9	a. Joseph
1.10	e. Jesus
1.11	c. Holy Spirit
1.12	Son, Jesus, save, sins
1.13	4
1.14	2
1.15	1
1.16	3
1.17	5
1.18	a. squirt
	b. squirrel
	c. square
1.19	yes
1.20	school
1.21	K
1.22	a. scarf
	b. scissors
	c. scooter
	d. scarecrow
	e. school
1.23	no
1.24	scissors

SELF TEST 1

1.01	e. engaged
1.02	a. manger
1.03	b. Holy Spirit
1.04	d. virgin
1.05	c. Gabriel
1.06	a virgin
1.07	King David
1.08	the Holy Spirit
1.09	a virgin
1.010	Jesus
1.011	God
1.012	engaged
1.013	God's Son
1.014	God
1.015	shepherds
1.016	she, son, name, save, sins

SECTION 2

2.1	God
2.2	Joseph
2.3	Nazareth
2.4	Mary, Joseph, and their family went to Jerusalem for the Passover.
2.5	Mary and Joseph were on their way back to their home in Nazareth.
2.6	Mary and Joseph looked all over the city of Jerusalem.
2.7	Mary and Joseph looked for Jesus for three days.
2.8	Jesus was listening to the teachers, asking and answering questions.
2.9	Mary and Joseph felt sad and worried.
2.10	2
	1
	4
	3
	1
	3
	4
	2
2.11	Examples: thinking, love of God, body, love of people
2.12	read books—wisdom
	study the Bible—favor with God
	run, eat, and sleep—stature
	be kind to others—favor with man
2.13	(go) (Joe) (snow) (low) (old) (rope) (doe)
2.14	Teacher check

SELF TEST 2

2.01	5
2.02	1
2.03	4
2.04	3
2.05	6
2.06	2
2.07	wisdom
2.08	stature
2.09	favor with God
2.010	favor with man
2.011	(God)
2.012	(a virgin)
2.013	(worried)
2.014	(wise)
2.015	(David)
2.016	Jesus, wisdom, stature, God, man

SECTION 3

3.1 thirty
3.2 God
3.3 John the Baptist
3.4 Son
3.5 yes
3.6 yes
3.7 yes
3.8 life
3.9 stories
3.10 commandments
3.11
2	baptized	2	manger
2	engaged	3	commandments
2	increased	2	stature
2	wisdom	2	virgin
		3	eternal

3.12 car/pen/ter
Naz/a/reth
fa/vor
wis/dom
3.13 Him
3.14 The sick people believed that Jesus was God's Son
3.15 To hear His stories. To be healed.
3.16 Jesus is God's Son.
3.17 a. way
b. truth
c. life
3.18 Father
3.19 a. sin
b. eternal
3.20 Jesus
3.21 forgive, eternal, life
3.22 power
3.23 Father
3.24 the Son of God (Lord)
3.25 Teacher check
3.26 (everyone)
3.27 (sin)
3.28 (the Savior)
3.29 (life)
3.30 (Man) (Savior) (Son of God)

SELF TEST 3

3.01 way
3.02 truth
3.03 life
3.04 Father
3.05 me
3.06 (Lord) (man) (Savior)
3.07 (way) (Son of God) (teacher)
3.08 (truth) (life)
3.09 (healer)
3.010 (saves) (heals)
3.011 (teaches) (loves) (gives wisdom)
3.012 (gives eternal life) (forgives sin)
3.013 wisdom
3.014 stature
3.015 favor—God
3.016 favor—man
3.017 follower of Jesus
3.018 to dip into water
3.019 rules to obey
3.020 never ending
3.021 John the Baptist
3.022 Jesus
3.023 God
3.024 Mary
3.025 Gabriel

SECTION 4

4.1   Jesus, disciples
4.2   Example: He kept the Passover with his disciples.
4.3   He would be killed.
4.4   that night or the next day
4.5   Jerusalem
4.6   Judas Iscariot
4.7   heaven
4.8   His followers
4.9   to make the mansions ready for His followers
4.10   happy
4.11   true
4.12   true
4.13   false
4.14   true
4.15   kiss
4.16   leaders
4.17   leaders
4.18   betrayed
4.19   Garden
4.20   sixteen
4.21   herself
4.22   fourteen
4.23   loudness
4.24   yourself
4.25   seventeen
4.26   softness
4.27   myself
4.28   sadness
4.29   sins
4.30   forgive
4.31   spear
4.32   Scriptures
4.33   1. three
         1. tomb
         2. spoke
         3. live
         4. rock
         5. disciples
4.34   3, 2, 1, 4
4.35   Teacher check

SELF TEST 4

4.01   a beautiful, large house
4.02   to give away to the enemy
4.03   went to heaven
4.04   knowledge and understanding
4.05   for man's sins
4.06   In, Father's, many, not, I, told, go, place, you
4.07   yes
4.08   no
4.09   no
4.010 yes
4.011 yes
4.012 yes
4.013 no
4.014 no
4.015 yes
4.016 yes
4.017 4
4.018 2
4.019 6
4.020 1
4.021 3
4.022 10
4.023 8
4.024 5
4.025 7
4.026 9

LIFEPAC TEST

1. Judas Iscariot
2. Mary
3. John the Baptist
4. Jewish leaders
5. Roman governor
6. 3
7. 1
8. 2
9. 5
10. 4
11. I, way, truth, life, Father
12. Bethlehem
13. Nazareth
14. Jerusalem
15. the Holy Spirit
16. talk to the teachers
17. life
18. stories
19. commandments
20. forgive, sin
21. give, eternal, life

ALTERNATE LIFEPAC TEST

1. Father's, many, I, you, go
2. wisdom
3. stature
4. favor with God
5. favor with men
6. Father in Heaven
7. God
8. Gabriel
9. disciples
10. believers in Jesus
11. 2
12. 3
13. 1
14. 5
15. 4
16. forgive sins
17. give eternal life
18. Jesus
19. Mary
20. John the Baptist
21. Joseph
22. shepherd

BIBLE 302

ALTERNATE LIFEPAC TEST

NAME _____

DATE _____

SCORE _____

Each answer = 1 point

Write the missing words.

1. "In my _____ house are _____ mansions; if it were not so, _____ would have told _____ . I _____ to prepare a place for you." John 14:2

Write four ways that Jesus grew as a boy.

2. _____

3. _____

4. _____

5. _____

Circle the right word.

6. Jesus went up to his _____ .
   a. disciples   b. Father in heaven   c. home in Nazareth

7. "This is my beloved Son, in whom I am well pleased," said _____ .
   a. Mary   b. John the Baptist   c. God

8. "You are highly favored, the Lord is with you, blessed are you among women," said _____ .
   a. Gabriel   b. Mary   c. John the Baptist

9. Jesus invited the _____ to the Last Supper.
   a. people of Nazareth   b. Jewish leaders   c. disciples

10. The people who will go to heaven are the _____ .
   a. belivers in Jesus   b. good people   c. club members

Number in the order that they happened in Jesus' life.

11. _____ grew in wisdom, stature, favor with God and man

12. _____ killed

13. _____ born sinless

14. _____ went up to heaven

15. _____ lived again

Write two things that only Jesus can do. (The first letters of each word have been given as clues.)

16. f_____ s_____

17. g_____ e_____ l_____

Draw a line to the right person.

18. God gave power to save   ●   John the Baptist

19. Mother of the Savior   ●   Joseph

20. Baptized Jesus   ●   shepherd

21. Earthly father to Jesus   ●   Jesus

22. Went to see Jesus when He was born ●   Mary

BIBLE 303

Unit 3: God's Plan for Joseph

TEACHER NOTES

MATERIALS NEEDED FOR LIFEPAC	
Required	Suggested
(None)	• Bible • banner paper • crayons • dictionary • drawing paper • pencil

ADDITIONAL LEARNING ACTIVITIES

Section 1: God Took Care of Joseph

1. Discuss these questions with your students.

   a. Why did Jacob make a coat for Joseph?

   b. How did Jacob's sons help him?

   c. Jacob taught his sons something very special. What was it?

   d. What does "jealous" mean?

   e. Can you think of a time when you felt jealousy? Tell me about it.

   f. Can you think of a time when you knew someone was jealous of you or of something you had? How did that person react?

   g. Tell me about Joseph's dream. What did it mean?

   h. Why do you think sheaves of grain were used as objects in the dream?

   i. What did Joseph's brothers say about his dream? How did they feel?

   j. How is this dream going to fit in with what is God's plan for Joseph's life? Based on this dream, what do you think is going to happen in Joseph's life?

   k. How did Joseph feel about his brothers? They were not very nice to him so why did Joseph feel this way?

   l. What does Joseph's attitude toward his brothers say to us and the way we should live our lives?

   m. Can you think of a time when someone was not very nice or friendly to you? How did you feel? What did you do? What should you do?

   n. What did Joseph's brothers do to him? Why did they do this?

   o. Did Joseph at first accept willingly what they did to him? How do you know?

   p. What changed Joseph's attitude about the pit?

   q. Who bought Joseph? Why? For how much?

r. Did the brothers tell the truth about what happened to Joseph? What did they tell Jacob?

s. What made Jacob believe what his sons told him?

2. Make a class mural depicting Joseph's life thus far. Include pictures drawn like those in LIFEPAC—Joseph, his family, his dream, and so on. The mural may be in the form of a timeline with additional pictures added in sequence after each unit is finished.

3. Have children think of all the things that show God's goodness and protection during trouble and problems. Have them draw pictures showing such. These may include such things as a doctor's help during illness, mother or father's support with a problem, a policeman's protection, or a teacher settling a dispute. These pictures may be captioned by the children and displayed around classroom.

4. Provide construction paper to each child with small picture of sheep to be cut out. Have students write the verse Romans 8:28 on the sheep and cut it out. Attach a piece of yarn to the sheep. These may be used as bookmarks. Talk about Romans 8:28 and also the significance of a sheep in Joseph's life. Discussion may lead to the symbol of a sheep for our life with God as our shepherd.

5. Start small individual dictionary booklets with words from the vocabulary section. This is a good reference for spelling and study at any time. The first entries would be beast, camel, jealous, rebuke, sheaf, sheaves, silver, and slave.

6. Play a dictionary game. To do this, provide each student with a dictionary. (Use the same kind, if possible.) Then, say one of the vocabulary words. When you say the word, the students are to find that word in the dictionary. The first person to find it must then:

   a. give the page number so the others can turn to that page,

   b. say the guide words on that page,

   c. spell the word,

   d. read the definition.

   Using the vocabulary words for each section will reinforce spelling, dictionary use, and the meanings of the words. This game may be used and expanded as new vocabulary words are added with each section of the LIFEPAC.

7. Play a class or family game of charades using the LIFEPAC vocabulary words. Write each word on a piece of paper and place in a container. Have each student or family member draw one word and act it out. Alternatively, instead of acting out each word, each word could be illustrated on a large easel of paper. People would then have to guess the vocabulary word from the drawing. Again, this game could be expanded as new vocabulary words are added with each LIFEPAC section.

Section 2: God Helped Joseph

1. Discuss these questions with your students.

   a. Where did the traders take Joseph? What did they do with him there?

   b. Tell about a long trip that you have taken. Did you get tired? Did you think it would last forever? Describe your feelings.

   c. Tell me about the life of a slave. Have you heard about slaves living in our country?

d. How did Joseph's life in Egypt differ from that of his life at home?

e. Joseph had much wealth in Egypt. Was he happy? Why not? Was he a good slave?

f. Did the people in Egypt love God? How do you know?

g. How did God reward Joseph for his trust in Him?

h. How did Potiphar know about Joseph's relationship with God?

i. What did Potiphar do for Joseph? Why?

j. Why was Joseph put into prison?

k. Do you like everything that happens to you?

l. Do you often wonder why things happen to you?

m. What do you do when sad or bad things happen to you?

n. What did God do for Joseph while he was in prison?

o. Tell me about the butler's dream. What did it mean?

p. Tell me about the baker's dream. What did it mean?

q. Why do you think God revealed to Joseph what the butler's and the baker's dreams meant?

r. Tell me about Pharaoh's dream. What did it mean?

s. How did the interpretation of the men's dreams help Joseph later?

t. Who told Pharaoh about Joseph and his ability to interpret dreams?

u. Who made Pharaoh's dream happen?

v. Was Joseph really able to tell what dreams meant? Who really was doing it?

w. What did Pharaoh do for Joseph? Why?

x. What was Joseph's job?

y. Does God always talk to us in our dreams?

z. Do you think that He does sometimes?

2. Write these words and names on the board:

> Joseph, slave, Pharaoh, Jacob, shepherd, butcher, Benjamin, brothers, Potiphar, butler, governor, traders

Play a word game. As you point to one word, go around the room calling on individual children to give a quick, one-word response that would go with the word you are pointing to. The responses must be in reference to the story of Joseph. Expect quick responses and discount more-than-one-word responses. Examples of responses might be these: Joseph—son, slave, godly, good, governor; brothers—cruel, jealous, shepherds; slave—Joseph, sold. This is a fun filler game at the end of the day or in those extra minutes.

3. Add to the word list—abandon, baker, butler, chariot, famine, governor, idol, prison, pyramid, shepherd, and tomb. These words are to be added to the individual dictionary booklets started in Section 1.

4. Have individual children work up oral reports on the different ways God talks to us—His Word, our parents, teacher, minister, and sometimes in dreams. Encourage reports to give personal experiences.

5. Have the child think of something that has happened to him. The child tells why he thinks God may have allowed it to happen. He tells the good outcome and shows that it was part of God's plan that all things work together for the good of them that love God. The teacher should look for complete sentences. The teacher should look for sufficient length of story so that it relates experiences and expresses original ideas that show thought.

6. Stress to the children that God loves us and has a plan for each one of us. Talk to them about the importance of trusting God, no matter what. Encourage prayer as a way of staying close to God, especially when life gets hard.

Section 3: God Watched over Joseph

1. Discuss these questions with your students.

    a. God watched over Joseph. What has happened thus far that shows you this statement is true?

    b. How does God watch over you? Tell me some ways or some things that have happened to you that prove to you that this is true?

    c. What is a famine? What happens during a famine?

    d. What did Jacob and his family do during the famine?

    e. Why was grain needed?

    f. Who in Jacob's family went to Egypt? What did they take with them?

    g. Who did they go to in Egypt?

    h. Did they know who he was?

    i. What did Joseph remember when he saw his brothers?

    j. Did Joseph show anger toward his brothers? Why not?

    k. What did Joseph tell his brothers to do?

    l. What did he do to one brother?

    m. Did the brothers understand what Joseph was doing?

    n. Why was Joseph doing all these things?

    o. Do you think that the brothers had changed? How do you know?

    p. What did Joseph tell his brothers about what they had done to him?

    q. What did Joseph do for his family?

    r. Why did all these things happen to Joseph?

    s. In what way could your life be like Joseph's?

2. As a group, rewrite the story of Joseph on a chart paper. Assign parts to each child and let them act out the story. Talk first about individual personalities of each character. This activity may be worked up into a play to be presented to another classroom.

3. Display pictures around the room from the story of Joseph. These may be blown up from the book or collected from another source. As a group, decide upon titles for the individual pictures and write these titles under the pictures.

4. Have a child find the story of Joseph in the Old Testament. Have him read this Scripture to the class from his Bible.

5. Have individual children work up a project and report on the importance of grain in our life. Show them how to get information from the library. They may bring in grain cereal, flour, animal grain feed, and so on, for a display. Talk about how each one of these is a grain we depend upon. Therefore, stress how important grain was to the people in Joseph's day and how we still depend upon it today—in many different forms.

6. A collection of recipes using grain could be compiled and used as a gift for a family member at Christmas or another holiday.

7. Add to the word list "abundant." This word should be added to the individual dictionary booklets started in Section 1.

8. Allow each student to choose his/her favorite character from the story of Joseph. Then, invite each student to impersonate that character. Other students or family members would then ask each student 20 questions and try to guess which character he/she is impersonating.

Administer the LIFEPAC Test.

> The test is to be administered in one session. Give no help except with directions.
> Evaluate the tests and review areas where the students have done poorly.
> Review the pages and activities that stress the concepts tested.
> If necessary, administer the Alternate LIFEPAC Test.

ANSWER KEYS

SECTION 1

1.1	twelve
1.2	Benjamin
1.3	loved
1.4	Joseph is the one with the multi-colored coat.
1.5	love God
1.6	eleven brothers
1.7	Joseph's father and mother
1.8	hated
1.9	Teacher check
1.10	No, Joseph's brothers took his coat.
1.11	Reuben
1.12	deep
1.13	well
1.14	Teacher check
1.15	yes
1.16	yes
1.17	no
1.18	yes
1.19	yes
1.20	Egypt
1.21	camels
1.22	Judah
1.23	silver
1.24	slave
1.25	brothers
1.26	Teacher check
1.27	Teacher check
1.28	beast
1.29	traders
1.30	brothers
1.31	Reuben
1.32	Joseph
1.33	twenty pieces of silver

SELF TEST 1

1.01	care for sheep
1.02	a coat
1.03	twelve
1.04	love
1.05	Jacob
1.06	Benjamin
1.07	Canaan
1.08	Reuben
1.09	Egypt
1.010	no
1.011	yes
1.012	no
1.013	no
1.014	yes

SECTION 2

2.1	Joseph's master
2.2	Egypt's king
2.3	beautiful house
2.4	blessed
2.5	all he owned
2.6	4, 1, 3, 2, 5
2.7	butler
2.8	baker
2.9	Joseph
2.10	Teacher check
2.11	king of Egypt
2.12	seven fat cows
2.13	seven fat heads of grain
2.14	God
2.15	God
2.16	yes
2.17	governor
2.18	thirty
2.19	Ephraim
2.20	records

SELF TEST 2

2.01	blessed
2.02	two
2.03	governor
2.04	no
2.05	yes
2.06	yes
2.07	no
2.08	yes
2.09	a. all things
	b. good
	c. love
2.010	God
2.011	3
2.012	1
2.013	2
2.014	4

SECTION 3

3.1 Jacob
3.2 Benjamin
3.3 to buy food
3.4 Joseph
3.5

/s/	/k/
recess	coat
peace	color
city	could
nice	cow
	camel
	because
	Jacob

3.6 field
3.7 chief
3.8 believed
3.9 piece
3.10 – 3.12 Teacher check
3.13 Joseph's silver cup
3.14

Across	Down
1. Simeon	1. donkeys
2. happy	2. cup
3. sacks	3. silver
4. Benjamin	4. Jacob

3.15 all things, good, love
3.16 Teacher check

SELF TEST 3

3.01 a. in all the world
3.02 c. to buy food
3.03 grain
3.04 Either order:
    a. silver
    b. Joseph's silver cup
3.05 after
3.06 after
3.07 before
3.08 before
3.09 before
3.010 a.
3.011 b.
3.012 a.
3.013 a.
3.014 b.
3.015 Teacher check

LIFEPAC TEST

1. yes
2. no
3. yes
4. yes
5. yes
6. yes
7. Joseph
8. Benjamin
9. coat
10. king of Egypt
11. time of no food
12. 3
13. 1
14. 2
15. 5
16. 4
17. love God
18. twelve
19. two
20. seven years of plenty and seven years of famine
21. leave prison in 3 days and be butler to Pharaoh again
22. jealous of him
23. help his family get food and a new home
24. "And we know that all things work together for good to them that love God, to them who are the called according to his purpose."
25. Examples; any order:
    a. God saved Joseph from the pit.
    b. God helped Joseph get out of prison.
    c. God brought Joseph's family to him.
26. Examples; any order:
    a. Joseph gave them grain.
    b. Joseph gave them homes.
    c. Joseph gave them clothing.
27. Example:
    God will take care of me as He took care of Joseph. God is able to protect me everywhere I am.

ALTERNATE LIFEPAC TEST

1. d. Benjamin
2. a. Jacob
3. b. pit
4. e. famine
5. c. Potiphar
6. 5
7. 2
8. 3
9. 1
10. 4
11. yes
12. yes
13. no
14. no
15. yes
16. no
17. "And we know that all things work together for good to them that love God, to them who are the called according to his purpose."
18. Examples; any order:
    a. God saved Joseph from the pit.
    b. God helped Joseph get out of prison.
    c. God brought Joseph's family to him.
19. Examples; any order:
    a. Joseph gave them grain.
    b. Joseph gave them homes.
    c. Joseph gave them clothing.
20. Example:
    God will take care of me as He took care of Joseph. God is able to protect me everywhere I am.
21. twelve
22. idols
23. governor
24. food
25. dreams
26. pit
27. sheep

BIBLE 303

ALTERNATE LIFEPAC TEST

NAME _____

DATE _____

SCORE _____

Each answer = 1 point

Draw a line to the correct word.

1.	Joseph's youngest brother	●	a	Jacob
2.	Joseph's father	●	b.	pit
3.	where Joseph was put	●	c.	Potiphar
4.	time of no food	●	d.	Benjamin
5.	Joseph's master in Egypt	●	e.	famine

Number the sentences in the order they happened.

6. _____ Joseph became governor of Egypt.

7. _____ Joseph was thrown into a pit.

8. _____ Joseph was sold as a slave.

9. _____ Joseph's father gave Joseph a coat of many colors.

10. _____ Joseph was put in prison.

Write *yes* or *no* before each sentence.

11. _____ Joseph's brother sold him to traders.

12. _____ Joseph's brothers came to buy grain from him.

13. _____ Joseph's brothers became slaves.

14. _____ Egypt had ten years of plenty and seven years of famine.

15. _____ Joseph told Pharaoh the meaning of his dreams.

16. _____ Joseph lived in Egypt all his life.

Write Romans 8:28 from memory.

17. _____

_____

_____

_____

_____

Answer these questions in good sentences.

18. In what three ways did God help Joseph?

a. _____

b. _____

c. _____

19. In what three ways did Joseph help his family?

a. _____

b. _____

c. _____

20. How is the story of Joseph helpful to you today?

_____

_____

_____

_____

_____

Circle the correct answer to complete each sentence.

21. Jacob had _____ sons.
  a. ten   b. eleven   c. twelve

22. In Egypt, most people prayed to _____ .
  a. Jesus   b. idols   c. God

23. Joseph became _____ of Egypt.
  a. prince   b. king   c. governor

24. Joseph's brothers came to Egypt for _____ .
  a. food   b. money   c. donkeys

25. Pharaoh wanted to understand his _____ .
  a. slaves   b. dreams   c. magicians

26. Joseph was thrown into a _____ .
  a. lake   b. pit   c. fire

27. Jacob owned many _____ .
  a. idols   b. sheep   c. pits

BIBLE 304

Unit 4: You Can Use the Bible

TEACHER NOTES

MATERIALS NEEDED FOR LIFEPAC	
Required	Suggested
(None)	• Bible • 3" × 5" index cards • banner paper • concordance dictionary • dowels, 6 to 10 inches long • paste • scissors

ADDITIONAL LEARNING ACTIVITIES

Section 1: Books of the Bible

1. Discuss these questions with your class.

    a. What does it mean to "love God with all your heart"?

    b. How will you act if you are wise?

    c. Who do you know that is wise?

    d. What will happen in our lives if we read the Bible often?

    e. What will happen if we seldom read the Bible?

    f. What does the word *Gospel* mean?

2. For reading integration, have class alphabetize the books of the Bible.

3. Learn the meaning of *paraphrase*. Write one of the Bible stories in your own paraphrased language.

4. Using the Bible as reference material, write a report on one of the prophets.

Section 2: Study of the Bible

1. Discuss these questions with your class.

    a. Why does God give commands?

    b. Why has God written promises in the Bible?

    c. Does God help us to obey His commands?

    d. What is the difference between studying the Bible and reading the Bible?

    e. Should a person have a regular time for reading the Bible?

2. Divide the class into little Bible Study groups. Have each group choose a passage of Scripture to study and share its lesson with the class.

3. Have a minister talk to the class about the importance of Bible study.

4. Find out what a Bible study leader does. Volunteer to lead the class in a Bible study.

5. Find out what a Bible concordance is and how to use one. Prepare notes on your findings to hand in to the teacher.

6. From Section 2 of the LIFEPAC, *How to read the Bible* can be extended for the student to express in his writing tablet many questions he has about Bible study. Some of these questions can be used later in a devotional study book the student can make. Some of the questions will be answered for the student as he continues the LIFEPAC study. The teacher checks to see depth of spiritual thought and inquiry. The teacher evaluates the student's grasp of the importance of reading the Word.

Section 3: Verses of the Bible

1. Discuss these questions with your class.

   a. Is it easy to memorize Bible verses?

   b. What would people do if they suddenly found out that in a month there would be no more Bibles?

   c. What is your favorite Bible verse?

2. Divide the class into two teams. Alternating teams and going person by person, see which team can name the most books in the Bible.

3. Let each student memorize a Bible verse and tell the class what the verse means.

4. Make a report on different words from the Bible. Tell what the word means, and in what Bible verses it appears. Use the Bible concordance.

5. Make a devotional notebook.

6. Start a card file of memorized verses.

Section 4: Time for the Bible

1. Discuss these questions with your class.

   a. How does learning God's Word help you to be obedient to Him?

   b. How does knowing and doing the will of God make one happy?

   c. What does it mean to "grow in the Lord"?

   d. How much time do you think you should spend each day with God?

   e. Is it possible for a person to pray constantly as one Bible verse says to do?

2. Sing Scripture choruses or listen to recordings of Scripture singing.

3. Have class plays with different children being detectives. Have the detectives interview different Bible characters.

4. Find out what the theme of each of Paul's Epistles is. Write a short paragraph about each one.

5. Make a map of Paul's missionary journeys.

Administer the LIFEPAC Test.

The test is to be administered in one session. Give no help except with directions.
Evaluate the tests and review areas where the students have done poorly.
Review the pages and activities that stress the concepts tested.
If necessary, administer the Alternate LIFEPAC Test.

ANSWER KEYS

SECTION 1

1.1	yes
1.2	no
1.3	yes
1.4	yes
1.5	yes
1.6	Bible
1.7	Scriptures
1.8	salvation
1.9	faith
1.10	sigh, high, flight, fright, fight, might
1.11	yes
1.12	no
1.13	sleigh, weigh, weight, neighbor
1.14	eigh
1.15	child, Holy Scriptures, make, wise, salvation, faith, Christ Jesus
1.16	yes
1.17	yes
1.18	yes
1.19	no
1.20	yes
1.21	Teacher check
1.22	2
1.23	39
1.24	32
1.25	Genesis
1.26	no
1.27	1,600
1.28	Teacher check
1.29	27
1.30	Gospels
1.31	Greek
1.32	8
1.33	Revelation
1.34	13
1.35	Acts
1.36	Teacher check
1.37	Teacher check

SELF TEST 1

1.01	Hebrew
1.02	thirty-nine
1.03	Greek
1.04	Genesis
1.05	thirty-two
1.06	eight or nine
1.07	life
1.08	twenty-seven
1.09	Paul
1.010	child
1.011	a. child
	b. holy
	c. wise
	d. faith
	e. Christ
	f. Jesus
1.012	NT
1.013	OT
1.014	OT
1.015	NT
1.016	OT
1.017	NT
1.018	OT
1.019	NT
1.020	OT
1.021	NT
1.022	OT
1.023	yes
1.024	no
1.025	yes

SECTION 2

2.1	Example: When was it written?
2.2	Example: Why was it written?
2.3	Example: Who read it first?
2.4	Teacher check
2.5	All, God, reproof, instruction
2.6	profitable
2.7	doctrine
2.8	reproof
2.9	righteousness
2.10	inspiration
2.11	correction
2.12	instruction
2.13	Examples:
	disciples—discipline
	Second Coming—stewardship
2.14	book
2.15	chapter
2.16	verse
2.17	word
2.18	Bible
2.19	dictionary
2.20	Bible
2.21	promises
2.22	commands
2.23	main ideas

SELF TEST 2

2.01	book
2.02	chapter
2.03	verse
2.04	word
2.05	dictionary
2.06	reproof
2.07	Holy Scriptures
2.08	instruction
2.09	righteousness
2.010	given
2.011	God
2.012	reproof
2.013	instruction
2.014	2 Timothy 3:16
2.015	doctrine
2.016	correction
2.017	profitable
2.018	Old Testament
2.019	New Testament
2.020	Paul
2.021	promises
2.022	commands
2.023	Job, Psalms, Proverbs, Ecclesiastes, Song of Solomon
2.024	Hosea, Joel, Amos, Obadiah, Jonah, Micah, Nahum, Habakkuk, Zephaniah, Haggai, Zechariah, Malachi
2.025	2 Timothy 3:16

SECTION 3

3.1	Psalm 119:11
3.2	2 Timothy 3:15
3.3	2 Timothy 3:16
3.4	Romans 15:4
3.5	sin
3.6	wise
3.7	God
3.8	hope
3.9	He wanted to know.
3.10	He heard it many times.
3.11	He read it many times.
3.12	He said it many times.
3.13	sin, afraid, Jesus, live
3.14	in/sect, ex/tra, in/to, traf/fic, ex/plain, in/vite, in/side, tur/tle, bal/loon
3.15	turtle
3.16	extra
3.17	traffic
3.18	inside
3.19	balloon
3.20	explain
3.21	into
3.22	insect
3.23	invite
3.24	Thy word have I hid in mine heart, that I might not sin against thee.

SELF TEST 3

3.01	memorize
3.02	Holy Scriptures
3.03	sin
3.04	inspiration
3.05	hope
3.06	word, have, I
3.07	hid, in, mine
3.08	heart, that, I
3.09	might, not, sin
3.010	against
3.011	yes
3.012	no
3.013	no
3.014	yes
3.015	yes
3.016	sin
3.017	afraid
3.018	Jesus
3.019	live
3.020	know it
3.021	hear
3.022	read
3.023	say
3.024	Acts 17:11
3.025	daily

SECTION 4

4.1
1. know
2. read
3. pray
4. write
5. time
6. obey
7. special
8. day

4.2 donkey, turkey, key, receive, monkey
4.3 ey
4.4 ei
4.5 Set a special time every day.
4.6 Pray for God to help you to know Him better.
4.7 Read His Word.
4.8 Write down what it means to you.
4.9 Talk to God in prayer.
4.10 Obey God.
4.11 yes
4.12 no
4.13 yes
4.14 yes

SELF TEST 4

4.01 New Testament
4.02 Word
4.03 heart
4.04 Old Testament
4.05 daily
4.06 A special time is a time alone with God
4.07 special time
4.08 Pray
4.09 Him
4.010 Read
4.011 Write
4.012 Talk
4.013 Obey
4.014 I want to learn about God.
4.015 I want to read the Bible.
4.016 I want to talk to God.
4.017 NT
4.018 OT
4.019 NT
4.020 NT
4.021 OT
4.022 NT
4.023 OT
4.024 NT
4.025 NT

LIFEPAC TEST

1. book
2. chapter
3. verse
4. word
5. in the back
6. main ideas
7. promises, commands
8. Job (or Psalms, Proverbs, Ecclesiastes, Song of Solomon)
9. Genesis
10. twenty-seven
11. eight or nine
12. thirty-nine
13. thirty-two
14. Old Testament
15. New Testament
16. Paul
17. New Testament
18. So you won't sin against God.
19. wise
20. God
21. special time
22. God
23. wrote it?
24. was it written?
25. was it written?
26. were the problems?
27. were they solved?
28. Genesis
29. yes

ALTERNATE LIFEPAC TEST

1. two
2. New Testament
3. Revelation
4. memorize it
5. Proverbs (or Job, Psalms, Ecclesiastes, Song of Solomon)
6. a "special time"
7. 11
8. Psalm
9. 119
10. in the Bible
11. God
12. Old Testament
13. memorize it
14. Genesis
15. Acts
16. New Testament
17. New Testament
18. wise unto salvation through faith which is in Christ Jesus
19. a special time every day
20. that God will help you to know Him better
21. His Word, the Bible
22. down what the Word means to you
23. to God in prayer
24. God
25. wrote the words
26. were they written
27. were they written
28. problems did the people face
29. were their problems solved

BIBLE 304

ALTERNATE LIFEPAC TEST

NAME _____

DATE _____

SCORE _____

23 / 29

Each answer = 1 point

Write the answers.

1. How many Testaments are in the Bible? _____

2. In which Testament are the thirteen letters written by Paul? _____

3. Which Bible book tells about Jesus' returning?_____

4. What do we do to learn a verse "by heart"? _____

5. What is one of the Old Testament books that teaches us to be happy?

   _____

6. What do you call a time alone with God? _____

7. In Psalm 119:11, which number is the verse number? _____

8. In Psalm 119:11, what tells the name of the book? _____

9. In Psalm 119:11, which number is the chapter? _____

10. Where are God's promises and commands written?

    _____

11. Who gave Scripture by inspiration? _____

12. In which Testament will you find Malachi 3:10? _____

13. How do you hide God's Word in your heart?

    _____

14. Which is the first book in the Bible? _____

15. Which New Testament book tells about church history and the Holy

Spirit? _____

16. 2 Timothy 3:16 is in which Testament? _____

17. Which Testament teaches about Jesus' life? _____

18. What does the Holy Scripture make you? _____

_____

Write six ways to have a "special time" with God.

19. Set _____

20. Pray _____

21. Read _____

22. Write _____

23. Talk _____

24. Obey _____

When you read your Bible, you need to find out what things?

25. Who _____?

26. To whom _____?

27. Where _____?

28. What _____?

29. How _____?

BIBLE 305

Unit 5: God Takes Care of His People

TEACHER NOTES

MATERIALS NEEDED FOR LIFEPAC	
Required	Suggested
(None)	• Bible • crayons • drawing paper

ADDITIONAL LEARNING ACTIVITIES

Section 1: God Cares for You

1. Differentiate between Elijah and Elisha in order to help students remember each one by writing their names on the chalkboard. Call for facts about each man and list them under the appropriate names.

2. Read Matthew 6:27–34 to the children to further illustrate Jesus' concern for all creatures.

3. Have children dramatize the LIFEPAC story "The Five Sparrows."

4. Have children work on a mural to illustrate the stories of Elijah and Elisha.

5. Students may draw pictures for the stories in Section 1 of the LIFEPAC. They may hang their pictures on the wall or bulletin board.

6. Students may use a concordance and check for references about children and God's care for them.

Section 2: God Guides and Protects You

1. Play the "Spider Web Game" with the children. Have one child be the spider. He will hold one end of the string. Ask questions about the Bible stories. After a student answers correctly, unroll string and have the student hold onto the string. Continue until all students are holding a part of the string and a big web has been formed.

2. Write Bible verses on paper. Mount them on heavier paper, cut the words apart and mix them up. Keep the verses in separate envelopes. Give students verses to put in the right order for a spare-time activity.

3. Stage a class play of the Shadrach, Meshach, and Abednego story. Some children can write the script; some can act in it. Present it for another class or for parents.

4. Have children read aloud the stories of the Israelites being guided by a cloud and a fire and Shadrach, Meshach, and Abednego being protected in the furnace. Use a children's Bible storybook.

5. Have children prepare reports on the Bible characters in the Section 2 stories.

6. Have children compose riddles to test the class on its knowledge of different people: Abednego, Meshach, Shadrach, Nebuchadnezzar, for example.

Section 3: God Blesses You

1. Conduct a discussion session contrasting the behaviors of Samuel and Samson. Guide the children to understand why God rewarded one man and not the other man.

2. For a free time activity, have the students find Bible verses telling of the importance of obeying God. Make a chart of these verses.

3. Have the children play "Bible Verse Hangman" in the following way: Choose two teams. On the board, draw enough spaces for all the letters of the chosen Bible verse. Between each word draw a slash line. Students guess letters that go on lines. A team gets a point for each correctly guessed letter.

4. Divide the class into three groups. Have each group prepare one of the Bible stories of Section 3.

5. A student may make a rebus story of a Bible verse or story by substituting pictures for some words.

6. Students may make a picture book for the LIFEPAC having each page be an illustration of one of the Bible stories in the LIFEPAC.

Administer the LIFEPAC Test.

> The test is to be administered in one session. Give no help except with directions.
> Evaluate the tests and review areas where the students have done poorly.
> Review the pages and activities that stress the concepts tested.
> If necessary, administer the Alternate LIFEPAC Test.

ANSWER KEYS

SECTION 1

1.1 The people were excited to see and hear Jesus.
1.2 Jesus spoke about God.
1.3 Jesus was happy to see the children.
1.4 ~~Nobody came to hear Jesus speak.~~
1.5 ~~The disciples were friendly to the children.~~
1.6 Jesus said "Let the children come to me."
1.7 Jesus loves you very much.
1.8 Teacher check
1.9 Teacher check
1.10 Example: God cares more for one person than for anything else in the world.
1.11 famine
1.12 Elijah
1.13 God
1.14 small stream
1.15 ravens
1.16 woman
1.17 loved
1.18 God
1.19 soul
1.20 life
1.21 taught
1.22 sought
1.23 night
1.24 caught
1.25 thought
1.26 fight
1.27 Teacher check
1.28 1. loves
2. oil
3. helped
4. Elisha
5. prayed
6. trouble

SELF TEST 1

1.01 no
1.02 yes
1.03 yes
1.04 no
1.05 yes
1.06 oil
1.07 children
1.08 Elisha
1.09 Elijah
1.010 God
1.011 money
1.012 pennies
1.013 disciples
1.014 children
1.015 stream
1.016 means that the people are hungry.
1.017 loves you more than all the sparrows.
1.018 were bought by Johnny.
1.019 were brought by the ravens.
1.020 wanted to see Jesus.
1.021 tell of God's love and help.

SECTION 2

2.1 "Happy is the man that findeth wisdom, and the man that getteth understanding."

2.2 4, 1, 2, 3

2.3
a. re turn
b. fel low
c. sta tion
d. riv er
e. sev en
f. lit tle
g. o pen
h. mid dle

2.4 prayed to statues made of stone and wood.

2.5 God.

2.6 refused to bow down and said they would only worship God.

2.7 not harmed.

2.8 worship God.

2.9 knives

2.10 wolves, thieves

2.11 calves

2.12 wives

2.13 He can help me make good decisions.

2.14 He will help me to be safe.

SELF TEST 2

2.01 chased Moses and the people.

2.02 saw a cloud.

2.03 led God's people through the sea.

2.04 were safe in the furnace.

2.05 was fed by ravens.

2.06 no

2.07 yes

2.08 no

2.09 yes

2.010 yes

2.011 yes

2.012 no

2.013 no

2.014 God

2.015 Moses

2.016 four

2.017 Egypt

2.018 fire

2.019 you

2.020 ravens

2.021 Elijah

2.022 sea

2.023 four

2.024 oil

2.025 hungry

SECTION 3

3.1	tightness
3.2	slowly
3.3	painful
3.4	forgetful
3.5	sugarless
3.6	quickly
3.7	He obeyed Eli. He worked hard and loved and obeyed God.
3.8	They disobeyed Eli. They did bad things. They stole and disobeyed God.
3.9	I can obey my parents and teachers. I can work hard in school. I can love God.
3.10	strong
3.11	cut
3.12	lion
3.13	jawbone
3.14	Delilah
3.15	cut
3.16	punished
3.17	Teacher check
3.18	friendly, suddenness, sugarless, tightly, beautiful, painful, fastness, deepness, immediately, thoughtful, sickness, suddenly, careful, slowly, sleepless, quickly, spotless
3.19	man, wisdom, man, understanding, 13
3.20	Lot and Abraham had men working for them who fought.
3.21	The men fought over grass and water for the animals.
3.22	Abraham had Lot choose the land he wanted.
3.23	Lot chose the best land.
3.24	God promised Abraham other good land.
3.25	Example: If I love God, He will reward me.
3.26	answers will vary
3.27	answers will vary
3.28	Teacher check
3.29	2, 2, 3, 1, 2, 3, 1
3.30	O O
	O N
	O O
	N N
	O O
	O O
	N O
	O

SELF TEST 3

3.01

Obeyed God:	Did not Obey God:
Samuel	Hophni
Solomon	Phinehas
Abraham	Samson
Elijah	Pharaoh
Elisha	
the widow	
Shadrach	
Meshach	
Abednego	
Moses	
Eli	

3.02	yes
3.03	no
3.04	no
3.05	no
3.06	yes
3.07	no
3.08	led people in desert
3.09	a strong man
3.010	a wise man
3.011	gave woman oil
3.012	was helped by God to give life to a boy
3.013	a small bird
3.014	Example: He protects me when I'm scared in the dark.
3.015	Example: He wants me to be nice and not fight.

LIFEPAC TEST

1. c. pots
2. d. Elijah
3. a. Elijah
4. c. the ravens
5. prophet
6. strong
7. God
8. children
9. Samson
10. punished
11. no
12. yes
13. no
14. yes
15. yes
16. Moses
17. furnace
18. wisdom
19. obey
20. punished

ALTERNATE LIFEPAC TEST

1. no
2. no
3. yes
4. yes
5. yes
6. obeyed
7. guides
8. ravens
9. widow
10. Elijah
11. Abraham
12. Samson
13. furnace
14. Moses
15. statues
16. God
17. children
18. Solomon
19. Samuel

BIBLE 305
ALTERNATE LIFEPAC TEST

NAME _____

DATE _____

SCORE _____

Each answer = 1 point

Write *yes* or *no*.

1. _____ Jesus was too busy to see the children.

2. _____ Pharoah's army killed Moses and the people with him.

3. _____ God gave Solomon the wisdom to be a good king.

4. _____ God punished Samson when he did not obey.

5. _____ God will take care of you if you love and obey Him.

Write the correct word or words in each blank.

6. God rewarded Samuel because he _____ .
   a. did not obey   b. obeyed

7. God protects and _____ you.
   a. makes fun of   b. guides

8. God cared for Elijah and sent _____ to feed him.
   a. three men   b. ravens

9. God cares about everyday matters because He helped a poor
   _____ .
   a. raven   b. widow

10. The boy was brought back to life by _____ .
   a. Elisha   b. Elijah

11. The fight over grass and water for animals was settled by

_____ .

   a. Abraham   b. Samson

Complete the sentences with the right words.

12. When his hair was cut, _____ became weak.
   a. Samuel   b. Samson   c. Moses   d. Abraham

13. Shadrach, Meshach, and Abednego were thrown into a

_____ .

   a. lion's den   b. deep pit   c. furnace   d. stream

14. God used a cloud to guide the people and _____ .
   a. Moses   b. Samson   c. Abraham   d. Solomon

15. King Nebuchadnezzar prayed to _____ .
   a. God   b. a golden calf   c. statues   d. men

Write the word from the list that belongs on each line.

children   Samuel
God   Solomon

16. You are protected by _____ .

17. Jesus loved the little _____ .

18. A man who was very wise was _____ .

19. A boy who went to help Eli the priest was _____ .

BIBLE 306

Unit 6: The Bible Is God's Word

TEACHER NOTES

MATERIALS NEEDED FOR LIFEPAC	
Required	Suggested
(None)	• Bible • writing tablets • Bible maps • extra nice writing paper • crayons, colored pencils, markers, or paint • dictionary

ADDITIONAL LEARNING ACTIVITIES

Section 1: God's Word Is Different

1. Discuss these questions with your class.

   a. Discuss with the class some of the writers of the various books of the Bible. Emphasize the role of the Holy Spirit and how He inspired these writers.

   b. Why did it take so many years for the Bible to be written?

   c. Who is the one true author of the Bible?

2. Introduce the children to the knowledge of different translations of the Bible. Use some of them for comparison with the King James language. A good parallel Bible may be useful in doing this.

3. Children may begin working on memorizing the books of the Bible. One good way of doing this is by singing a song with the books of the Bible in order.

4. Children may draw and color Bible maps, using maps in their Bibles as resource material.

5. Children may begin research into great Bible translators such as Tyndale or Wycliff.

6. Children may find out about the work of such groups as the American Bible Society and the Gideons. Perhaps a member of one of these groups might speak to the class about the work they do.

7. See Bible 303 Section 1, activities 5, 6, and 7 for ideas on how to learn and reinforce vocabulary words for each section of the LIFEPAC.

8. Scramble the vocabulary words and have the students write them in alphabetical order.

9. Have the students write one synonym and/or one antonym for each vocabulary word.

10. For each section of the LIFEPAC, allow the children to retell the story in their own words. Narration is a wonderful way to determine comprehension on the student's part.

11. For review, prior to each test, have each student write several questions about what has been covered. (These can be short answer questions, true/false questions, or multiple choice questions.) Allow each student to quiz the class and see who can answer the most questions correctly.

Section 2: God's Word Is Preserved

1. Discuss these questions.

    a. What are some ways that God has preserved His Word over the years?

    b. What were the Dead Sea Scrolls? Where and when were they found?

    c. What was the Law of Moses? Who gave the Law to Moses?

    d. How did God feel about Josiah?

    e. How could you know if a person is reading the Bible?

    f. Does God reward people for reading the Bible? If so, in what ways?

    g. Name some examples from history of how God's word survived attacks.

2. Children may make covers to protect their Bibles.

3. Children may learn and sing the song, "The B-I-B-L-E."

4. Children may present reports from their research about great translators and the American Bible Society and the Gideons.

5. Children may do research about the authors of different Bible books.

6. Have the children do an oral or written report about what they can do to help preserve God's Word. Discuss ideas in class first to help get the students started. The children might also discuss this with their parents and/or pastors to help get ideas.

Section 3: God's Word Changes Lives

1. Discuss these questions with your class.

    a. Why was the king so willing to allow Nehemiah to go and rebuild the wall?

    b. How did prayer help Nehemiah?

    c. Why was Nehemiah so careful to always give God credit and glory?

    d. Discuss the details of the job of cupbearer and why it was important for this man to be trustworthy.

    e. What role does fasting have in the life of a believer? How can fasting make a difference? Discuss other Biblical examples from the Old and New Testaments where the people fasted and what happened.

    f. Why is it important to persevere and not give up? What might have happened if Nehemiah had not encouraged the people and they all quit? Encourage the children to persevere.

    g. Discuss in more depth the vocations of priest and scribe in Old Testament times. Why were these jobs important? In what ways did they contribute to the life and spiritual well-being of the community?

    h. Discuss in more depth how the Word of God changed the lives of Nehemiah, Ezra, the Jews, and the Apostle Paul and others. Ask the students how the Word has impacted their lives. Encourage sharing.

2. Make a mural of the rebuilding of the wall of Jerusalem.

3. Let the children take turns being Ezra as he read the Law of Moses.

4. Make a chart of the Ten Commandments. Use a "stone tablet" design.

5. Make a list of words that describe Nehemiah. Also Ezra and Paul.

6. Let each child be a scribe! Allow each child to choose a favorite verse or small portion of Scripture. Have them copy it on nice paper. Encourage them to do it with no mistakes. If possible, obtain a book with good pictures of old Scriptures which have been copied by hand. Display the finished work on a class bulletin board.

7. Using a good Bible map, locate Philippi and Colosse. Talk about these and other churches Paul founded on his missionary journeys. Use colorful push pins to mark where these cities would be on the Bible map.

Section 4: God's Word Has Promises

1. Discuss these questions with your class.

   a. Should we only think about Jesus' birth on Christmas?

   b. Who was Isaiah?

   c. Why is it important for someone to keep his promises?

   d. What part of the Bible did Jesus read?

   e. What promises of God do you know?

2. Draw pictures of some of God's promises. See if the other children can guess which promise is being illustrated.

3. Enact different parts of Jesus' life. Group the class for this activity. Explain to the class what a passion play is.

4. Make a card file of God's promises. Each day, allow one student to choose a card from the file and read it aloud to the class.

5. Make a banner or poster of the Bible verse John 3:16 or some other Bible verse used in this LIFEPAC.

Administer the LIFEPAC Test.

> The test is to be administered in one session. Give no help except with directions.
> Evaluate the tests and review areas where the students have done poorly.
> Review the pages and activities that stress the concepts tested.
> If necessary, administer the Alternate LIFEPAC Test.

ANSWER KEYS

SECTION 1

1.1	book
1.2	God's loving plan of salvation
1.3	Jesus Christ
1.4	one writer
1.5	forty-one
1.6	no
1.7	no
1.8	yes
1.9	no
1.10	yes

1.11

Across	Down
1. consistent	4. God
2. sin	5. inspiration
3. years	6. Jesus

SELF TEST 1

1.01	many
1.02	foretold
1.03	occupations
1.04	book
1.05	God's loving plan of salvation
1.06	forty-one
1.07	1,600
1.08	Holy Spirit
1.09	Bible
1.010	yes
1.011	yes
1.012	yes
1.013	yes
1.014	no

SECTION 2

2.1	not pass away
2.2	thousands
2.3	endureth for ever
2.4	scribes
2.5	preserve
2.6	Dead Sea Scrolls
2.7	King of Judah
2.8	priest of the temple
2.9	secretary
2.10	lost Book of the Law
2.11	in Jerusalem
2.12	Teacher check
2.13	4
2.14	3
2.15	2
2.16	1
2.17	5

SELF TEST 2

2.01	Jesus
2.02	men in France
2.03	scribes
2.04	Peter
2.05	Constantine
2.06	Josiah
2.07	yes
2.08	yes
2.09	yes
2.010	yes
2.011	no
2.012	finds the Book of the Law
2.013	main character of the Bible
2.014	destroyed many Bibles
2.015	inspired the Bible
2.016	thousands
2.017	preserve
2.018	Dead Sea Scrolls
2.019	God's loving plan of salvation
2.020	It has endured and survived many attacks.

SECTION 3

3.1	a.	Nehemiah
3.2	c.	trust
3.3	b.	sad
3.4	a.	a letter
3.5	c.	soldiers
3.6		no
3.7		no
3.8		yes
3.9		yes
3.10		rebuild the city wall
3.11		priest and scribe
3.12		the Law of Moses
3.13		with the poor
3.14		His Word
3.15		Teacher check
3.16		Teacher check
3.17	c.	Jew
3.18	b.	Pharisee
3.19	a.	churches
3.20	c.	Timothy

SELF TEST 3

3.01	to give hope and support to someone
3.02	to go without food
3.03	to treat in a mean way
3.04	one who ministers before God
3.05	one who writes and teaches
3.06	Nehemiah
3.07	Paul
3.08	the king
3.09	Ezra
3.010	Timothy
3.011	no
3.012	no
3.013	yes
3.014	no
3.015	yes
3.016	the gates and walls
3.017	who is great and terrible
3.018	is your strength
3.019	by inspiration of God
3.020	live in you

SECTION 4

4.1   Yes
4.2   Isaiah 7:14
4.3   Yes
4.4   Either or both of these: The Gospels of Matthew and Luke; Luke 2:7
4.5   God
4.6   good news to the poor
4.7   Any one of these:
        He preached good news to the poor.
        He set people free who were prisoners of sin.
        He healed people from sickness.
        He healed broken hearts.
4.8   in the synagogue
4.9   yes
4.10 Jonah
4.11 the Holy Spirit
4.12 He was taken up to heaven. A cloud hid Him from the disciples.
4.13 two angels
4.14 They said that Jesus would come back in the same way the disciples saw Him go into heaven.
4.15 yes
4.16 yes
4.17 4, 2, 5, 1, 3

SELF TEST 4

4.01   yes
4.02   no
4.03   yes
4.04   yes
4.05   yes
4.06   no
4.07   no
4.08   no
4.09   yes
4.010 yes
4.011 a. scripture
          b. God
          c. doctrine
          d. correction
          e. instruction
4.012 book
4.013 a. God's loving plan of salvation
4.014 b. Jesus Christ
4.015 c. Paul
4.016 a. Ezra
4.017 c. Isaiah
4.018 a. Matthew and Luke
4.019 b. God
4.020 a. Jonah
4.021 b   angels

LIFEPAC TEST

1. yes
2. yes
3. yes
4. yes
5. no
6. yes
7. yes
8. yes
9. yes
10. yes
11. foretold
12. occupations
13. book
14. God's loving plan of salvation
15. Dead Sea Scrolls
16. it has endured and survived many attacks
17. Paul
18. Ezra
19. Matthew and Luke
20. God
21. forty-one
22. 1,600
23. Holy Spirit
24. Bible
25. Nehemiah
26. Ezra
27. The Bible is consistent even though it had many writers over many years. The Bible endures and survives attacks. God's Word in the Bible changes lives. God's promises in the Bible are fulfilled.
28. 5
29. 2
30. 1
31. 3
32. 4

ALTERNATE LIFEPAC TEST

1. b. Paul
2. f. Nehemiah
3. a. Ezra
4. e. Bible
5. g. Josiah
6. c. two angels
7. d. Jesus
8. thousands of
9. God's loving plan of salvation
10. preserve
11. is your strength
12. Jew
13. Jesus Christ
14. cloud
15. a. scripture
    b. God
    c. teaching
    d. correction
    e. training
16. no
17. yes
18. yes
19. no
20. yes
21. yes
22. yes
23. no
24. 5
25. 1
26. 3
27. 4
28. 2

BIBLE 306

ALTERNATE LIFEPAC TEST

NAME _____

DATE _____

SCORE _____

Each answer = 1 point

Draw a line to the correct word or words.

1. God's Word changed his life   ●   a.   Ezra

2. Rebuilt the walls of Jerusalem   ●   b.   Paul

3. priest and scribe   ●   c.   two angels

4. contains God's Word   ●   d.   Jesus

5. preserved a lost book of the Bible   ●   e.   Bible

6. spoke to disciples about Jesus   ●   f.   Nehemiah

7. "My words will not pass away."   ●   g.   Josiah

Circle the correct answer.

8. God's Word in the Bible has endured for _____ years.
   a. a hundred   b. five hundred   c. thousands of

9. The main theme of the Bible is _____ .
   a. the story of Nehemiah and Ezra
   b. how the world was created
   c. God's loving plan of salvation

10. God helped _____ His Word over many years.
    a. Moses make up   b. preserve   c. change

11. The joy of the Lord _____ .
    a. is hard to find
    b. comes from a good joke
    c. is your strength

12. Paul was born a _____ .
    a. Pharisee   b. Jew   c. Gentile

13. The main character of the Bible is _____ .
    a. Jesus Christ   b. Abraham   c. Isaiah

14. When Jesus went up to heaven, a _____ hid Him from the disciples.
    a. blanket   b. cloud   c. tree

Write the correct word in each blank.

15. "All a. _____ is inspired by

    b. _____ and profitable for

    c. _____ , for reproof, for

    d. _____ , and for

    e. _____ in righteousness…"

                              (2 Timothy 3:16)

Write *yes* or *no* before each sentence.

16. _____ The story of Jesus' birth is found in Matthew and Mark.

17. _____ Most books have one writer.

18. _____ The true author of the Bible is God.

19. _____ Nehemiah was a scribe for the king.

20. _____ God's Word will always endure.

21. _____ A Greek king tried to destroy the Old Testament.

22. _____ The Holy Spirit inspired the Bible.

23. _____ The Bible is not consistent because it had many writers over many years.

Put these events in the correct order. Number them 1 to 5.

24. _____ The Dead Sea Scrolls were found in caves in Israel.

25. _____ Hilkiah finds the lost Book of the Law.

26. _____ Paul writes letters to Timothy.

27. _____ Men in France say the Bible will pass away in 100 years.

28. _____ Jesus goes up into heaven.

BIBLE 307

Unit 7: Archaeology and the Bible

TEACHER NOTES

MATERIALS NEEDED FOR LIFEPAC	
Required	Suggested
(None)	• Bible • Bible maps • crayons • colored pencils

ADDITIONAL LEARNING ACTIVITIES

Section 1: Preparing the Hunt

1. Discuss these questions with your class.

    a. What differences are there between ruins and artifacts?

    b. Do you think God has a hand in preserving certain things from old cultures?

    c. How is your present-day culture different from the culture of Ur, Abraham's hometown?

    d. Does the way a person worships tell anything about the way he lives?

2. Divide the class into little groups and have each group act out a day's work for an archaeologist.

3. Prepare a time capsule of artifacts from the classroom.

4. Use the encyclopedia to do research about noted archaeologists.

5. Find out the difference between an archaeologist and an anthropologist.

Section 2: Understanding the Search

1. Using the chalkboard, make a list of the ways archaeology supports the authenticity of the Bible.

2. List reasons that cities might become buried one on top of another, forming tels.

3. List questions students may have concerning Bible times and peoples for which archaeology might provide answers.

4. Have students make pictures of Ur.

5. Have students draw pictures showing how Rahab's house could have been built on a wall.

6. Have students do research on how much education and training one needs to be an archaeologist.

7. Make a diorama of the walls of Jericho.

Section 3: Joining in the Search

1. Discuss these questions with your class.

    a. Why is it hard for some people to believe the Bible?

    b. What is faith?

    c. Could the Bible be a handbook for an archaeologist?

    d. Why was King Solomon's request so pleasing to God?

    e. What caused Bible lands to change over many years?

    f. What changes are going on in your community that make the scene different in appearance from one year to the next?

2. Have someone who has been to the Holy Land speak to the class.

3. Show a film or video on Bible lands.

4. Make a list of tools that the archaeologist uses.

5. Find out what modern-day countries compose the former Mesopotamia.

Administer the LIFEPAC Test.

The test is to be administered in one session. Give no help except with directions.
Evaluate the tests and review areas where the students have done poorly.
Review the pages and activities that stress the concepts tested.
If necessary, administer the Alternate LIFEPAC Test.

ANSWER KEYS

SECTION 1

1.1 Hint: The boat shows they sailed and probably traded. The picture of the cart and horses shows the way they traveled. The woman shows how they looked and dressed. The writing shows the type of language they wrote. The bowl shows that they painted and gives an example of something they ate with.

1.2 archaeologist —— a person who studies what early man made and left behind

1.3 ruins — the things that man made and left behind

1.4 ancient — very, very old

1.5 artifacts — what is left after something is torn down or broken in pieces

1.6 They look for handmade things used long ago, like pots and pans, streets, and houses.

1.7 They show how people lived and worked years ago.

1.8 a. toothbrush
b. knives
c. paintbrush

1.9 b. pictures are taken
c. notes are made
d. it is measured

1.10 a. pieces pottery together
b. studies his notes
c. asks questions

1.11 Answers will vary.
Hint: I worked so hard to learn about a new people from the past and to enjoy the excitement of telling the world about them.

1.12 a. cutting
b. digger
c. saddest
d. hoping
e. trader

1.13 first clues to the past—old stories

1.14 one city built upon another—tell

1.15 between the Tigris and Euphrates rivers—Mesopotamia

1.16 mystery bricks—strange marks and writings

1.17 Teacher check

1.18 yes

1.19 yes

1.20 yes

1.21 no

1.22 1

1.23 4

1.24 2

1.25 5

1.26 3

SELF TEST 1

1.01 yes
1.02 no
1.03 yes
1.04 yes
1.05 no
1.06 They tell them how ancient people lived and worked.
1.07 Example:
The reward is to tell the world about unknown people.
1.08 They showed people had lived there as the Bible said. They helped archaeologists find ancient cities.
1.09 Over the years, the clay houses washed down and new ones were built on top.
1.010 a. study artifacts
b. dig into ruins
d. learn about the past
1.011 a. measures it
b. digs it out
c. takes a picture
d. brushes away the dirt
1.012 b. Ur
c. Babylon
d. garden of Eden

SECTION 2

2.1 yes
2.2 yes
2.3 no
2.4 yes
2.5 yes
2.6 a. sim-ple
b. Bi-ble
c. puz-zle
d. an-kle
e. can-dle
f. set-tle
2.7 gaps
2.8 happened
2.9 a. Old Testament
b. New Testament
2.10 scrolls
2.11 They told us what life was like between the Old and New Testaments.
2.12 Answers will vary. Hint: I would really be surprised to hear the breaking pots. When I would see the scrolls, I would tell the people of my town about the strange caves.
2.13 Jericho had two walls around it. Houses were built to join them.
2.14 a. photo
b. laugh
c. enough
d. rough
2.15 dead, steady, breath
2.16 yes
2.17 no
2.18 yes
2.19 yes
2.20 yes

SELF TEST 2

2.01 archaeologist
2.02 artifact
2.03 scroll
2.04 true
2.05 God
2.06 400
2.07 archaeology
2.08 ancient
2.09 Ur
2.010 yes
2.011 no
2.012 yes
2.013 no
2.014 yes
2.015 no
2.016 a. were in a cave
b. tell of Jewish life
d. fill a gap
2.017 a. had two walls
b. had houses on the walls
d. walls were destroyed by God
2.018 It gives us artifacts that prove that the places were there.
2.019 By telling us what happened in the missing years.
2.020 By helping us understand how God made things happen.

SECTION 3

3.1 yes
3.2 no
3.3 a. able to be plowed
b. able to be answered
c. act of agreeing
d. act of enjoying
3.4 a. rocks in layers
b. animal prints
c. mixed-up rocks
3.5 a. in the Bible
b. by archaeologists
c. by our Earth
d. by clay tablets
3.6 a. like a baby
b. belonging to Jews
c. going toward the sky
d. going outward
3.7 no
3.8 yes
3.9 garden of Eden
3.10 God
3.11 the Flood
3.12 Solomon
3.13 Any order:
a. Nazareth
b. Bethlehem
3.14 Lazarus
3.15 city
3.16 third
3.17 a. still there
b. ruins
c. called by a new name
3.18 b. is near Jerusalem
c. may be where Christ died
d. looks like a skull
3.19 a. Skull Hill
b. the garden grave
c. cities Jesus visited
3.20 Drawings will vary

SELF TEST 3

3.01 archaeologist
3.02 tell
3.03 Dead Sea Scrolls
3.04 Jericho
3.05 yes
3.06 yes
3.07 no
3.08 yes
3.09 yes
3.010 no
3.011 yes
3.012 yes
3.013 yes
3.014 They wrote stories and drew pictures of them showing they knew Bible stories.
3.015 mixed-up rocks, animal prints
3.016 lived
3.017 true

LIFEPAC TEST

1.	things man made	artifacts
2.	archaeologist's work room	laboratory
3.	a way of life	culture
4.	rolls of paper for writing	scrolls
5.	to make from nothing	create
6.	yes	
7.	yes	
8.	yes	
9.	yes	
10.	no	

11. a. search for cities
    b. dig into ruins
    c. learn about the past
12. a. proving that it's true
    b. filling gaps
    c. explaining puzzles
13. a. Ur
    b. Jericho
    c. Eridu
14. By finding artifacts and digging in Bible sites, archaeology shows us many things about the way places looked and how people lived. Archaeology also fills in the gaps in Bible history and explains puzzling events like Jericho.
15. laboratory
16. tablet

ALTERNATE LIFEPAC TEST

1. no
2. yes
3. yes
4. yes
5. yes
6. no
7. a. scroll
8. d. culture
9. c. laboratory
10. b. tells
11. a. proving is true
    b. explaining puzzles
12. c. search for cities
    d. dig into ruins
13. Archaeology unearths artifacts from Bible times. These artifacts help us to know how Bible people lived and what their towns and cities were like.
14. artifact
15. ruins
16. archaeologist

BIBLE 307

ALTERNATE LIFEPAC TEST

NAME _____

DATE _____

SCORE _____

14
18

Each answer = 1 point

Write *yes* or *no* before each sentence.

1. _____ People couldn't write in Moses' day.

2. _____ Archaeology proves what the Bible says is true.

3. _____ Abraham's city, Ur, worshiped many gods.

4. _____ Skull Hill may be where Christ was buried.

5. _____ God used human writers to write His words in the Bible.

6. _____ Archaeologists study arches.

Draw lines to match.

7. roll of paper for writing ● a. scroll

8. everything about the way a people lives ● b. tells

9. archaeologist's work room ● c. laboratory

10. cities built one on top of each other ● d. culture

Circle all the answers that are true.

11. Archaeology helps you understand the Bible by _____ .
   a. proving it true
   b. explaining puzzles
   c. copying it
   d. selling it

12. Archaeologists _____ .
   a. break artifacts
   b. write scrolls
   c. search for cities
   d. dig into ruins

Answer this question.

13. How does archaeology help us to understand the people and places of the Bible?

   _____

   _____

   _____

Write the missing word.

14. Anything made by man is an _____ .

15. What are left after something is torn down are the _____ .

16. A scientist who studies the past is an _____ .

BIBLE 308

Unit 8: God Gave Us the Need for Friends

TEACHER NOTES

MATERIALS NEEDED FOR LIFEPAC	
Required	Suggested
(None)	• Bible • magazines • scissors

ADDITIONAL LEARNING ACTIVITIES

Section 1: We Need Love

1. Discuss these questions with your class.

   a. Why did God give the Ten Commandments?

   b. How can we show love to God?

   c. How is Jesus the best example of love?

   d. Why did Jesus tell us to "love your enemies"?

   e. What is the most loving thing you can do for a friend?

2. Draw pictures of the Garden of Eden and Adam and Eve.

3. Draw pictures to illustrate each of the Ten Commandments.

4. Make banners or posters with the theme of love.

5. Do research in the Bible to discover God's teachings about how we are to love each other.

Section 2: We Need Friendship

1. Discuss these questions.

   a. Is it possible to become God's enemy?

   b. What chapter in the Bible is called the "Love Chapter"?

   c. Is it possible to be a friend to a person without showing him love?

   d. What does it mean to "forgive and forget"?

   e. Do some people deserve to have friends more than other people do?

2. Have the class act out the stories of Ruth and Naomi and David and Abigail.

3. Have the class read in unison 1 Corinthians chapter 13.

4. Have students make a list of their friends. Have them make another list of people they should befriend. Beside those names, have them write what they could do to win each person's friendship.

Section 3: Others Need Our Friendship

1. Discuss these questions with your class.

    a. What does it mean to love God completely?

    b. Do people sometimes worship idols that cannot be seen?

    c. Why does God need our love?

    d. Why do we need God's love?

    e. Does obeying your parents tell you that you love them?

    f. In the Christian way, what is the difference between liking someone and loving him?

2. Make table favors for a retirement home or a hospital.

3. Send an email to the son or daughter of a missionary that your church supports.

4. Have students begin a prayer diary.

5. Write a paper explaining the sentence, "God Is Love."

Administer the LIFEPAC Test.

The test is to be administered in one session. Give no help except with directions.
Evaluate the tests and review areas where the students have done poorly.
Review the pages and activities that stress the concepts tested.
If necessary, administer the Alternate LIFEPAC Test.

ANSWER KEYS

SECTION 1

1.1 garden
1.2 Either order:
  a. plants
  b. animals
1.3 alone
1.4 Either order:
  a. friend
  b. helper
1.5 love
1.6 friends
1.7 ribs
1.8 love
1.9 man
1.10 Either order:
  a. think
  b. talk
1.11 a. 5
  b. 2
  c. 1
  d. 3
  e. 4
1.12 no
1.13 yes
1.14 no
1.15 no
1.16 a. second
  b. sixth
  c. seventh
  d. first
  e. ninth
  f. tenth
  g. eighth
1.17 Examples:
  a. Sue was fourth in line.
  b. Sam is in the eighth grade.
1.18 a. first
  b. second
  c. third
  d. fifth
1.19 a. thirtieth
  b. fortieth
  c. fiftieth
  d. sixtieth
1.20 a. sixty
  b. seventy
  c. eighty
  d. ninety

1.21 Examples:
  a. Sixty people were here.
  b. Eighty buttons spilled on the floor.
1.22 a. safety
  b. specialty
1.23 Examples:
  a. Safety is important.
  b. A policeman's specialty is safety.
1.24 Across
  1. love
  2. father
  3. kill
  4. David
  Down
  5. Saul
  6. Jonathan
  7. friend
  8. brave
1.25 no
1.26 yes
1.27 yes
1.28 no
1.29 yes
1.30 no
1.31 "Thou shalt not kill."
1.32 treat people with love
1.33 a. Exodus
  b. Ten
1.34 a. God
  b. other
1.35 a. neighbor
  b. thyself
1.36 Either order:
  a. sheep
  b. servants
1.37 a. churlish
  b. hateful or unfriendly
1.38 food
1.39 killing
1.40 a. "Honour thy father and thy mother."
  b. "Thou shalt not kill."
  c. "Thou shalt not commit adultery."
  d. "Thou shalt not steal."
  e. "Thou shalt not bear false witness against thy neighbor."
  f. "Thou shalt not covet."

1.41 a. tenth
        b. shalt not covet

1.42 a. eighth
        b. shalt not steal

1.43 a. ninth
        b. shalt not bear false witness

1.44 "For even the Son of man came not to be ministered unto, but to minister, and to give his life a ransom for many."

1.45 Teacher check

SELF TEST 1

1.01 The sixth commandment   e. thou shalt not kill.

1.02 Whoever hates someone   d. is as bad as a murderer.

1.03 It is not good   a. for man to be alone.

1.04 Husbands and wives share   b. a special kind of love.

1.05 as much as yourself

1.06 honor and respect

1.07 Saul

1.08 seventh

1.09 Nabal

1.010 the right way

1.011 they both loved God

1.012 we do not love God or others

1.013 Jonathan

1.014 God

1.015 Jesus

1.016 God

1.017 Jesus or God

1.018 God

SECTION 2

2.1   Enoch
2.2   Adam and Eve
2.3   Abraham
2.4   Enoch
2.5   sin
2.6   walked
2.7   believed
2.8   a. love
          b. obey
2.9   a. 1
          b. 3
          c. 1
          d. 1
          e. 2
2.10 a. transplant
          b. transport
          c. transatlantic
2.11 Teacher check
2.12 a. 4
          b. 2
          c. 5
          d. 3
          e. 6
2.13 Proverbs 17:17a, "A friend loveth at all times..."
2.14 a. kept David from killing in anger or doing something wrong
          b. she brought gifts of friendship
2.15 Teacher check
2.16 a. told
          b. put
          c. hurried
          d. cutters
2.17 Teacher check
2.18 a. Solomon listened to the problems of his people.
          b. He turned the people to God.
          c. He prayed for his people.
2.19 choose your friends
2.20 food
2.21 Temple

2.22 war
2.23 Examples:
          friendship
          share Jesus with a friend
2.24 Teacher check
2.25 a. friend
          b. forgives
2.26 a. Jesus
          b. friend
2.27 b. forgives
          c. forgets
2.28 Teacher check
2.29 sinners
2.30 friends
2.31 die
2.32 sinned
2.33 leave
2.34 brother
2.35 God
2.36

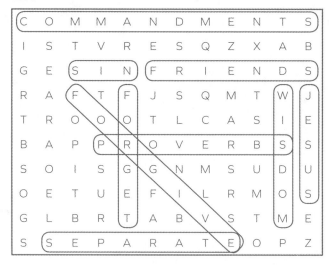

SELF TEST 2

2.01	close
2.02	pleased
2.03	believed
2.04	friend
2.05	Ruth
2.06	covet
2.07	proverbs
2.08	please
2.09	heart
2.010	example
2.011	brother
2.012	helped
2.013	no
2.014	yes
2.015	yes
2.016	yes
2.017	yes

2.018	Jonathan	a.	David
2.019	sinners	d.	Jesus
2.020	no one	e.	Nabal
2.021	his people	b.	King Solomon
2.022	Eve	f.	Adam
2.023	Naomi	c.	Ruth
2.024	everyone	g.	God
2.025	commandment		
2.026	murderer		
2.027	lie		
2.028	ransom		

SECTION 3

3.1 Teacher check

3.2
a. shalt have no other gods before
b. shalt not make unto thee any graven
c. shalt not take the name of the Lord God in
d. the sabbath day to keep it

3.3
a. 1
b. 4
c. 3
d. 2
e. 4
f. 3
g. 1

3.4 Teacher check

3.5
a. 1 John 4:21, "And this commandment have we from him, That he who loveth God love his brother also."
b. John 15:14, "Ye are my friends, if ye do whatsoever I command you."

3.6 Teacher check

3.7 b. you will love your brother also.

3.8 a. you are a liar.

3.9 d. by obeying His commandments.

3.10 e. by giving.

3.11 c. through us.

3.12 Teacher check

3.13 one's own written name

3.14 Examples:
John upended the box and sat on it.
The car drove uphill
The crowd was in an uproar.
The rain upset his plans.

3.15
a. punches
John threw five punches.
b. bosses
The three bosses went to work.
c. foxes
The foxes are asleep.

SELF TEST 3

3.01   no
3.02   yes
3.03   no
3.04   yes
3.05   yes
3.06   no
3.07   no
3.08   Luke 10:27
      a. Lord
      b. God
      c. heart
      d. all
      e. soul
      f. mind
      g. neighbor
3.09   Proverbs 17:17a
      a. friend
      b. times
3.010 John 15:13
      a. love
      b. man
      c. this
      d. down
      e. life
      f. his
3.011 4 or fourth
      a. sabbath
      b. holy

3.012 6 or sixth
      kill
3.013 8 or eighth
      not
3.014 9 or ninth
      a. shalt
      b. false
      c. thy
3.015 5 or fifth
      a. father
      b. mother
3.016 10 or tenth
      shalt not
3.017 7 or seventh
      a. shalt not
      b. adultery
3.018 1 or first
      a. have
      b. gods
3.019 2 or second
      a. make
      b. any
      c. image
3.020 3 or third
      a. name
      b. lord
      c. God

LIFEPAC TEST

1. yes
2. no
3. yes
4. no
5. no
6. yes
7. yes
8. no
9. no
10. no
11. e. And this commandment have we from Him, that he who loveth God loveth his brother also.
12. d. Ye are my friends, if ye do whatsoever I command you.
13. b. Thou shalt love thy neighbor as thyself.
14. c. A friend loveth at all times.
15. a. Thou shalt not steal.
16. helper
17. respect
18. wrong
19. protect
20. hate
21. example
22. proverbs
23. friends
24. commandments
25. have friends or show love of Jesus or please God

ALTERNATE LIFEPAC TEST

1. f. John 15:14
2. a. Mark 10:45
3. d. Proverbs 17:17a
4. c. 1 John 4:21
5. e. Exodus 20:16
6. yes
7. yes
8. yes
9. no
10. no
11. yes
12. no
13. yes
14. no
15. Example:
   He always loves me and teaches me to love others.
16. friends
17. murderers
18. times
19. yourself
20. God
21. Commandment
22. wrong
23. problems
24. respect
25. example

BIBLE 308

ALTERNATE LIFEPAC TEST

NAME _____

DATE _____

SCORE _____

Each answer = 1 point

Draw lines to match the verses.

1. Ye are my friends, if ye do whatsoever I command you. ●

2. For even the Son of man came not to be ministered unto, but to minister, and to give his life a ransom for many. ●

3. A friend loveth at all times. ●

4. And this commandment have we from Him, that he who loveth God love his brother also. ●

5. Thou shalt not bear false witness against thy neighbor. ●

a. Mark 10:45

b. Proverbs 18:24b

c. 1 John 4:21

d. Proverbs 17:17a

e. Exodus 20:16

f. John 15:14

Answer *yes* or *no*.

6. _____ To hate is to break the sixth commandment.

7. _____ Animals do not think as man does.

8. _____ People who have true love give to others.

9. _____ A good friend will do the wrong with his friends.

10. _____ Adam said, "It is good for me to be alone."

11. _____ The greatest love is to lay down your life for your friends.

12. _____ Adam made the woman.

13. _____ Jesus came to give His life as a ransom for many.

14. _____ You can love God without loving others.

Complete this sentence.

15. My best friend is Jesus because _____

_____ .

Write the correct word on the line.

commandment	God	respect
yourself	example	murderers
times	friends	problems
wrong		

16. God wants us to have _____ .

17. People who hate others are called _____ .

18. A friend loves at all _____ .

19. You are to love your neighbor as much as _____ .

20. After sin came into the world, men were no longer close friends of

_____ .

21. To hate is to break the sixth _____ .

22. Abigail was a friend to David when she kept him from doing

_____ .

23. Solomon listened to people when they had _____ .

24. A wife should _____ her husband.

25. One who shows how to act is an _____ .

BIBLE 309

Unit 9: God's People Help Others

TEACHER NOTES

MATERIALS NEEDED FOR LIFEPAC	
Required	Suggested
(None)	• Bible • crayons • heavy, colored paper • glitter • 3" x 5" file cards for verses • colored tissue paper • pipe cleaners • egg cartons • clay • pebbles • tempera paint colors • assorted small boxes

ADDITIONAL LEARNING ACTIVITIES

Section 1: Who Am I to Care For?

1. Discuss these questions with your class.

    a. Are people sometimes afraid to be friendly? Why?

    b. How would you feel if your family moved to a different town and you began attending a new school?

    c. Are children always friendly to each other in Sunday school?

    d. When someone new visits your class, what should you do?

    e. Is it easier for grownups or children to make friends?

2. Sing "What a Friend We Have in Jesus."

3. Have children list new ways to be friendly.

4. Have children make a book file of books read about children in other countries or cultures.

5. Make a scrapbook filled with pictures depicting friends and friendship.

Section 2: Why Should I Serve Others?

1. Discuss these questions with your class.

    a. If people truly loved their brothers as themselves, what would the world be like?

    b. Are there people you should love in God's way, but not be friends with them?

    c. How does Jesus help us live for Him?

    d. Do all people need to ask God for forgiveness?

    e. Will going to church every Sunday make a person a Christian?

    f. Why is it easier to be friends with some people than it is with other people?

    g. How does a person become friends with God?

2. Have children take a field trip to a retirement home.

3. Have each child "adopt" a younger student and be a big brother or sister to the younger child.

4. Have children learn new Spanish vocabulary words and make a file of those they have learned.

5. Have children make a file of Bible verses which speak of love.

Section 3: Who Will Care for Me?

1. Discuss these questions with your class.

    a. How do you become God's child?

    b. What people has God provided to take care of you?

    c. What is meant by "peace of mind"?

    d. Are even adults God's children?

    e. How can other people know that you are a Christian?

2. Have children write stories describing God and His love and care for His children.

Administer the LIFEPAC Test.

The test is to be administered in one session. Give no help except with directions.
Evaluate the tests and review areas where the students have done poorly.
Review the pages and activities that stress the concepts tested.
If necessary, administer the Alternate LIFEPAC Test.

ANSWER KEYS

SECTION 1

1.1 *Jesucristo*
1.2 life
1.3 alone
1.4 every language
1.5 Jesus Christ
1.6 kindly
1.7 tenderhearted
1.8 forgive
1.9 because God has forgiven me
1.10 for Christ's sake
1.11 share
1.12 forgive
1.13 serve
1.14 be kind to the unkind
1.15 tell others about Jesus
1.16 show God's love
1.17 wear
1.18 flower
1.19 read
1.20 blew
1.21 sew
1.22 too
1.23 know
1.24 toe
1.25 bear
1.26 Serve

1.27 Share
1.28 Tell others about Jesus
1.29 Forgive
1.30 Be kind to the unkind
1.31 Show God's love
1.31 – 1.37 Examples:
1.32 I can set the table for mother.
1.33 I can share my toys with my friends.
1.34 I can take a friend to Sunday school.
1.35 I can forgive my brother when he hits me.
1.36 I can give an apple to the boy who always picks on me.
1.37 I can wash Daddy's car.
1.38 Example:
She believed God helped her.
1.39 no
1.40 Rosa trusted in *Jesucristo* as her Savior
1.41 no
1.42 Rosa prays to God through *Jesucristo*.
1.43 Rosa thanks God through *Jesucristo*.
1.44 no
1.45 Rosa loves God through *Jesucristo*.
1.46 Rosa belongs to the family of God through *Jesucristo*.
1.47 Teacher check

SELF TEST 1

1.01   a. be
        b. kind
        c. tenderhearted
        d. forgiving
        e. another
        f. God
        g. Christ's
        h. you
        i. 32

1.02   good people   everyone   Christians

1.03   Christians

1.04   *Jesucristo*   Jesus

1.05   Christians   people

1.06   love   serve   forgive

1.07   pray

1.08   Jesus Christ

1.09   serve

1.010 share

1.011 forgive

1.012 be kind to the unkind

1.013 tell others about Jesus

1.014 show God's love to others

1.015 Love God

1.016 Pray to God

1.017 Thank God

1.018 Belong to the family of God

SECTION 2

2.1   Beloved, if God so loved us, we ought also to love one another.

2.2   at school

2.3   help her with her schoolwork

2.4   She did not want to give up her free time to help Rosa.

2.5   Sally

2.6   Rosa forgave Sally or Rosa invited Sally to her home.

2.7   Teacher check

2.8   yes

2.9   no

2.10 yes

2.11 no

2.12 yes

2.13 yes

2.14 yes

2.15 no

2.16 yes

2.17 halt

2.18 welt

2.19 lisp

2.20 salt

2.21 felt

2.22 crisp

2.23 grasp

2.24 belt

2.25 fault

2.26 wasp

2.27 a. kind
        b. God
        c. you

2.28 a. God
        b. love

2.29 Example:
So He can love them through us.

SELF TEST 2

2.01 Christians
2.02 ought
2.03 Jesus
2.04 kind
2.05 God
2.06 loves
2.07   a. Beloved
     b. God
     c. loved
     d. love
     e. another
2.08 God loves   d. me
2.09 to work for others   e. serve
2.010 tenderhearted   a. feeling kind
                         toward others
2.011 eternal   b. lasts forever
2.012 *Jesucristo*   g. Jesus Christ
2.013 Mexico   f. a country south of
                         the United States
2.014 ought   c. to have a duty
2.015 Any order:
     a. serve
     b. share
     c. forgive
     d. tell others about Jesus
     e. be kind to the unkind
     f. show God's love
2.016 because God hath forgiven me

SECTION 3

3.1 1
3.2 4
3.3 2
3.4 3
3.5 nothing
3.6 everything
3.7 by prayer
3.8 to ask for something
3.9 thanksgiving
3.10 God
3.11 nothing
3.12 everything
3.13 prayer
3.14 thanksgiving
3.15 requests
3.16 Teacher check
3.17   a. through others
     b. through joy and peace of mind
     c. through rewards in heaven
3.18 Any order:
     a. about trusting in Jesus as her Savior
     b. about being a child of God
     c. that God loves and cares for His children
     d. that God loved her mother, too
3.19   a. receive
     b. believe
     c. relief
     d. thief
     e. brief
     f. chief
     g. tried
     h. view
3.20 believe
3.21 view
3.22 thief
3.23 receive
3.24 chief
3.25 tried
3.26 relief
3.27 brief
3.28 fudge
3.29 smudged
3.30 lodge
3.31 budge
3.32 dodge
3.33 budget
3.34 through others
3.35 through joy and peace of mind
3.36 through rewards in heaven

3.37   Across
1. *Jesucristo*
2. everything
3. Jesus
4. papa
5. smile
6. share
7. love
8. king
9. pray
Down
1. joy
6. sin
8. kind
9. poor
10. thanks
11. supplication
12. others
13. God

3.38   gifts from friends   through others
3.39   in reading God's Word   joy and peace of mind
3.40   trusting in Jesus as   joy and peace of personal Savior   mind
3.41   in friends who pray for   through others them
3.42   in knowing God cares   joy and peace of for them   mind
3.43   in having eternal life   rewards in heaven

SELF TEST 3

3.01   requests   things that are asked for
3.02   supplication   to ask for something
3.03   eternal   lasts forever
3.04   careful for nothing not to worry
3.05   God's family   Christians
3.06   a. careful
           b. everything
           c. prayer
           d. thanksgiving
           e. your
           f. known
           g. God
           h. 4:6
3.07 – 3.09 Any order:
3.07   through others
3.08   through joy and peace of mind
3.09   through rewards in heaven
3.010 true
3.011 false
3.012 false
3.013 true
3.014 false
3.015 true
3.016 true
3.017 false
3.018 true
3.019 false
3.020 1 John 4:11
3.021 Ephesians 4:32
3.022 Ephesians 4.32
3.023 Philippians 4:6–7
3.024 Ephesians 4.32
3.025 Philippians 4:6–7
3.026 Example: When we went on a trip and had a flat tire, God sent people along to help us.

LIFEPAC TEST

1. a. if
   b. God
   c. loved
   d. ought
   e. to
   f. love
   g. another
2. a. serve them
   b. love them with God's love
   c. tell others about Jesus
   d. share with them
   e. not a true statement
   f. forgive them
   g. be kind to the unkind
   h. not a true statement
3. a. belong to the family of God
   b. love God
   c. not a true statement
   d. not a true statement
   e. thank God for being saved
   f. have eternal life
   g. not a true statement
4. true
5. true
6. true
7. true
8. true
9. true
10. true
11. true
12. Christians
13. ought
14. loves
15. eternal
16. thanksgiving
17. a. English
    b. Spanish

ALTERNATE LIFEPAC TEST

1. eternal
2. prayer
3. everything
4. a. English
   b. Spanish
5. joy
6. heaven
7. a. belong to the family of God
   b. love God
   e. thank God for being saved
   f. have eternal life
8. b. tell God about all things
   c. be kind to unkind people
   e. thank God when they ask Him for something
   h. "love thy neighbor as thyself"
9. a. kind
   b. another
   c. forgiving
   d. God
   e. sake
   f. you
10. true
11. true
12. false
13. false
14. true
15. true
16. false
17. true

BIBLE 309

ALTERNATE LIFEPAC TEST

NAME _____

DATE _____

SCORE _____

Each answer = 1 point

Write a word from the list to complete each sentence.

English	heaven	prayer
eternal	joy	Spanish
everything		

1. Life that lasts forever is _____ .

2. Christians can talk to God through _____ .

3. Christians should pray about _____ .

4. Rosa could not speak much a. _____ because she
   spoke b. _____ .

5. God gives peace of mind and _____ .

6. God will give rewards in _____ .

Draw a line under all true statements.

7. Only Christians can _____ .
   a. belong to the family of God
   b. love God
   c. belong to a big church
   d. sing about Jesus
   e. thank God for being saved
   f. have eternal life
   g. look like Christians

8. God wants Christians to _____ .
   a. worry about unkind people
   b. tell God about all things
   c. be kind to unkind people
   d. not forgive a mean person
   e. thank God when they ask Him for something
   f. make others do what they want
   g. give others what they deserve
   h. "love thy neighbor as thyself"

Complete Ephesians 4:32 by writing the missing words.

9. "And be ye a. _____ one to b. _____ ,
   tenderhearted, c. _____ one another, just as
   d. _____ for Christ's e. _____ hath forgiven
   f. _____ ."

Write *true* or *false*.

10. _____ One way God takes care of you is through others.

11. _____ All people are God's creation.

12. _____ Christians should always have their own way.

13. _____ Everyone is a Christian.

14. _____ God loves you.

15. _____ You are a Christian by faith in Jesus.

16. _____ God loves everyone, so people do not need to love
   each other.

17. _____ Jesus is God and is the Son of God.

BIBLE 310

Unit 10: God's Word, Jesus, and You

TEACHER NOTES

MATERIALS NEEDED FOR LIFEPAC	
Required	Suggested
(None)	• Bible • crayons • concordance • dictionary

ADDITIONAL LEARNING ACTIVITIES

Section 1: The Word of God

1. Discuss these questions with your class.

    a. What is meant by the "still, small voice of God"?

    b. Do miracles happen in this day?

    c. How does knowing the story of Abraham help you learn about God?

    d. Is it necessary to understand God's commands in order to obey him?

    e. Do you always understand why your parents tell you to do something?

    f. If we forget about God, does He forget about us?

    g. What does the Bible mean when it says that we should obey God rather than men?

    h. Why was God pleased with Solomon's request?

2. Have children write about the gift or talent they think God has given them.

3. Have a contest or quiz to see who can list the most books of the Old Testament (or New Testament).

4. Call out a Bible book. Point to the student who can identify whether it is in the Old or New Testament.

5. Read the Bible for ten minutes each day. Keep a journal of Scripture study.

6. Try to memorize the books of the Bible.

Section 2: The Son of God Makes the Word Known

1. Discuss these questions with your class.

    a. What do we mean when we say that Jesus rose again in glory?

    b. How did Jesus make the prophecy of Isaiah come true?

    c. What kind of a childhood do you think Jesus had?

    d. How did Jesus make it possible for all people to be part of God's family forever?

    e. Why was Jesus willing to suffer such great pain?

2. Read the Biblical account of Jesus calling His twelve disciples. Have children draw individual pictures of each of the disciples.

3. Have children draw a fold-out picture account of Jesus' life.

4. Have a child read the same story in several different Gospels. Have the student write a comparison of the different accounts as written by different men.

5. Memorize the names of the Twelve Disciples.

Section 3: The Children of God

1. Discuss these questions with your class.

   a. How can you love your neighbor as yourself?

   b. How can you love your enemy?

   c. Have you ever had to suffer for Jesus?

   d. Can you tell a way you have served God?

   e. How do you become a part of God's heavenly family?

   f. Will God punish us for our sins? Why or why not?

   g. What does this verse mean: "We ought to obey God rather than men"?

2. Prepare a class choral reading of one of the Psalms.

3. Discuss with children the symbolism of the lily at Easter.

4. Memorize one of the Psalms.

5. Find out what a creed is. Memorize a familiar creed (for example, the Apostles' Creed).

Administer the LIFEPAC Test.

The test is to be administered in one session. Give no help except with directions.
Evaluate the tests and review areas where the students have done poorly.
Review the pages and activities that stress the concepts tested.
If necessary, administer the Alternate LIFEPAC Test.

ANSWER KEYS

SECTION 1

1.1   No one   has seen God.
1.2   God created   the universe.
1.3   Abraham heard   God speak.
1.4   Isaac was   Abraham's son.
1.5   Abraham and
          Sarah   had a son.
1.6   The birth of Isaac   was a miracle.
1.7   Israelites
1.8   God
1.9   rules
1.10 Exodus
1.11 Commandments
1.12 (leaf) (read) (deep) (free) (he) (revealed)
          (believe) (tree) (feet) (me)
1.13 no
1.14 yes
1.15 yes
1.16 no
1.17 yes
1.18 by throwing them into the fiery furnace
1.19 The one true God protected Shadrach,
          Meshach, and Abednego.
1.20 Example:
          stories of Moses, Abraham, prophecy of
          Isaiah
1.21 Example:
          story of Jesus' life
1.22 telling what will happen before it happens
1.23 (blow) (thrown) (toe) (goat) (float) (tow)
1.24 King Solomon loved   God.
1.25 God gave Solomon   a gift.
1.26 King Solomon's story   is in the Old
                                    Testament.
1.27 King Solomon was   a wise judge.
1.28 yes
1.29 no
1.30 yes
1.31 yes
1.32 no
1.33 yes
1.34 Example:
          many people
1.35 Holy Spirit
1.36 Example:
          so everyone would know about God
1.37 scribes
1.38 forty

1.39 scrolls
1.40 prophecy
1.41 yes
1.42 yes
1.43 no
1.44 yes
1.45 no
1.46 no
1.47 Any order:
          Matthew, Mark, Luke, and John
1.48 Example:
          He told people about Jesus and helped start
          churches.
1.49 Teacher check
1.50 Teacher check

SELF TEST 1

1.01	no
1.02	yes
1.03	no
1.04	yes
1.05	yes
1.06	no
1.07	God gave King Solomon his wish.
1.08	Abraham's son was named Isaac.
1.09	Shadrach, Meshach, and Abednego walked in the fire.
1.010	Long ago the Bible was written on scrolls. God's word.
1.011	Scribes copied
1.012	Jesus'
1.013	life
1.014	doctor
1.015	Gospels
1.016	Abraham
1.017	Isaac
1.018	Commandments
1.019	prophet
1.020	churches
1.021	about Jesus' life
1.022	He had a vision. Jesus spoke to him.
1.023	Example: wisdom or knowledge
1.024	so that he could be a fair and good king
1.025	Either order: a. Old Testament b. New Testament

SECTION 2

2.1	exciting
2.2	Jesus
2.3	Joseph
2.4	angel
2.5	Bethlehem
2.6	shepherds
2.7	Teacher check
2.8	Teacher check
2.9	Any order: a. gold b. frankincense c. myrrh
2.10	Teacher check
2.11	yes
2.12	no
2.13	yes
2.14	no
2.15	yes
2.16	He was a carpenter.
2.17	twelve years
2.18	in the Temple
2.19	talking to the teachers
2.20	a. sought b. I c. Father's d. 2:49
2.21	baptized
2.22	disciples
2.23	miracles
2.24	thirty
2.25	a. way b. truth c. life d. man e. Father f. me g. 14:6
2.26	(make) (day) (baby) (way) (feign) (manger) (sleigh) (eight) (hay)
2.27	to celebrate Passover
2.28	They took Him and crucified Him.
2.29	He rose from the dead.
2.30	Easter
2.31	up to heaven on a cloud
2.32	Example: He died for me. He saved me from sin.
2.33	Teacher check
2.34	Teacher check

SELF TEST 2

2.01	yes
2.02	no
2.03	yes
2.04	no
2.05	yes
2.06	yes
2.07	no
2.08	no
2.09	no
2.010	no
2.011	Example: in a manger in Bethlehem
2.012	the shepherds and the wise men
2.013	The angel told them.
2.014	baptized
2.015	God
2.016	Isaiah
2.017	teachers
2.018	holiday
2.019	Bible
2.020	angel
2.021	miracles
2.022	rules
2.023	carpenter

SECTION 3

3.1	a.	joyful
	b.	Lord
	c.	lands
3.2	a.	Bless
	b.	Lord
	c.	soul
	d.	name
3.3	a.	thanks
	b.	Lord
	c.	good
	d.	mercy
3.4	a.	thing
	b.	praise
	c.	Lord
	d.	Lord
3.5	Teacher check	
3.6	Teacher check	
3.7	Love your neighbor	as yourself.
3.8	The Lord's prayer is	in the Gospel of Matthew.
3.9	God should be	first in your life.
3.10	We should love	our enemies.
3.11	God listens to	our prayers.
3.12	a.	un-, reason, -able
	b.	pre-, determin(e), -ed
	c.	de-, part, -ment
	d.	un-, bear, -able
	e.	un-, selfish, -ness
	f.	un-, kind, -ness
	g.	un-, fashion, -able
	h.	dis-, interest, -ed
	i.	un-, happ(y), -ness
3.13	Examples: pray, sing, smile, be kind, be cheerful, help others	
3.14	Teacher check	
3.15	yes	
3.16	no	
3.17	yes	
3.18	yes	
3.19	no	
3.20	God	
3.21	neighbor	
3.22	mansions	
3.23	Examples: sad, ashamed, sorry	
3.24	Examples: pray, ask for forgiveness	

SELF TEST 3

3.01 King Solomon   had great wisdom.
3.02 Jesus' twelve followers were called
                                   disciples.
3.03 You belong to the   family of God.
3.04 The Ten
          Commandments are   God's rules.
3.05 David wrote   the Psalms.
3.06 no
3.07 yes
3.08 yes
3.09 no
3.010 yes
3.011 no
3.012 yes
3.013 yes
3.014 Example:
          An angel told her.
3.015 Example:
          to praise God
3.016 The Lord's Prayer
3.017 Examples:
          be happy, helpful, kind, loving
3.018 Sarah
3.019 Mary
3.020 Jesus
3.021 scroll
3.022 praise
3.023 Matthew
3.024 New
3.025 enemies

LIFEPAC TEST

1. Mary
2. God
3. God
4. to the Temple in Jerusalem
5. He rose from the dead.
6. They brought gifts to the baby Jesus.
7. Example: many people; about forty writers
8. to praise God
9. one who dies for God
10. yes
11. yes
12. no
13. no
14. yes
15. no
16. The Psalms were written   to praise God.
17. The shepherds went to   Bethlehem.
18. Prophecy means   telling what is going to happen.
19. King Solomon had   great wisdom.
20. About forty men   wrote the Bible.
21. Jesus died for   our sins.
22. Jesus lived in   the city of Nazareth.

ALTERNATE LIFEPAC TEST

1. yes
2. no
3. no
4. yes
5. yes
6. yes
7. no
8. f. telling what is going to happen.
9. b. our sins.
10. a. praise.
11. d. the universe.
12. c. walked in the fire.
13. e. Gospels.
14. Jesus went to Jerusalem for the Passover. He went to the Temple to talk with the teachers about God.
15. Either order:
    a. Old Testament
    b. New Testament
16. David wrote the Psalms to praise God.
17. King Solomon asked for wisdom to be a good king and to judge his people fairly.
18. Jesus rose again in glory.
19. I would read the good news of Jesus.
20. John the Baptist
21. Easter
22. A martyr is someone who is killed because he loves God.

BIBLE 310

ALTERNATE LIFEPAC TEST

NAME _____

DATE _____

SCORE _____

18

23

Each answer = 1 point

Answer *yes* or *no*.

1. _____ The Lord's Prayer is found in the New Testament.

2. _____ Sometimes God does not keep His promises.

3. _____ Abraham was the father of Isaiah.

4. _____ It is important to obey your heavenly Father.

5. _____ Jesus had twelve disciples.

6. _____ The birth of Isaac was a miracle.

7. _____ The Bible has six parts.

Draw lines to complete the sentences.

8. *Prophecy* means ●

9. Jesus died for ●

10. The Psalms are Bible poems of ●

11. God created ●

12. Shadrach, Meshach, and Abednego ●

13. Matthew, Mark, Luke, and John are called the ●

a. praise.

b. our sins.

c. walked in the fire.

d. the universe.

e. Gospels.

f. telling what is going to happen.

Write the answers to the questions on the lines.

14. Where did Jesus go when He was twelve years old?

_____

_____

15. What are the two parts of the Bible?

a. _____

b. _____

16. Why did David write the Psalms? _____

17. Why did King Solomon want wisdom?

_____

_____

18. What happened three days after Jesus died?

_____

19. What would you read in the Gospels?

_____

20. Who baptized Jesus? _____

21. What day of the year is the happiest? _____

22. What is a martyr? _____

_____